CW00937789

OSPREY COMBAT AIRCRAFT • 98

A-10 THUNDERBOLT II UNITS OF OPERATION *ENDURING FREEDOM*
2002-07

SERIES EDITOR: TONY HOLMES

OSPREY COMBAT AIRCRAFT • 98

A-10 THUNDERBOLT II UNITS OF OPERATION *ENDURING FREEDOM* 2002-07

GARY WETZEL

OSPREY
PUBLISHING

Front Cover
Flying A-10A 78-0597, Maj Andrew Stone departed Bagram AB, Afghanistan on 30 October 2006 as 'Tusk 43'. Along with his wingman, Maj Reid Rasmussen, they were initially assigned to an area in southern Afghanistan. However, the two pilots from the 75th EFS were soon re-tasked to support troops-in-contact near Marah. Earlier that day Special Forces OD-A Team 316, its JTAC ('Mastiff 10') and a group of Afghan National Army soldiers had been ambushed by a large Anti-Coalition Militia (ACM) force. One American had been killed and the team had been separated, with one group effecting a CASEVAC and the other group fighting its way to higher ground to escape withering heavy machine gun and RPG fire that was mainly coming from a large grove of trees that separated the two teams by nearly a kilometre.

'Mastiff 10' began asking for immediate gun runs on the grove, and both teams began popping smoke to mark their positions. Green smoke drifted up from the location of the group that had called for the CASEVAC, while red smoke identified the spot of 'Mastiff 10'. After several strafing runs to quieten the enemy down, Maj Stone and his wingman began a search for reported ACM reinforcements. Unknown to him, the decision had been made for the teams to link back up. The only way to accomplish that was to go back into the valley and pass through the grove again.

'We received a call for immediate fire when we were about seven miles west', Maj Stone explained, 'and checking the grid coordinates "Mastiff 10" gave me, I realised they were on the move and were back in the grove. As I arrived overhead, I looked down and could see the world kind of exploding. I initially had no idea where the "friendlies" were, but they immediately popped more smoke and gave me a good reference. I turned and rolled in, choosing to make a low-angle strafe so as to put the rounds on target and reduce bullet dispersion, thus preventing any possibility of fratricide.'

For 23 minutes Maj Stone and his wingman provided support to OD-A Team 316, each pilot making 13 strafing passes to push back ACM **forces. Gun runs were made as close as 40 m from 'Mastiff 10' at altitudes as low as 100 ft, and more than 2000 rounds of 30 mm ammunition were expended. Four Mk 82 airbursts, one GBU-12 LGB and six white phosphorous rockets were also employed. For his actions that day, Maj Andrew Stone was awarded the Distinguished Flying Cross with Valor (*Cover art by Gareth Hector*)**

First published in Great Britain in 2013 by Osprey Publishing
Midland House, West Way, Botley, Oxford, OX2 0PH
4301 21st Street, Suite 220B, Long Island City, NY, 11101, USA

E-mail; info@ospreypublishing.com

Osprey Publishing is part of the Osprey Group

A CIP catalogue record for this book is available from the British Library

ISBN: 978 1 78096 304 4
e-book PDF ISBN: 978 1 78096 305 1
e-pub ISBN: 978 1 78096 306 8

Edited by Tony Holmes
Cover Artwork by Gareth Hector (www.garethhector.co.uk/aviation-art/)
Aircraft Profiles by Jim Laurier
Index by Michael Forder
Originated by PDQ Digital Media Solutions
Printed in China through Asia Pacific Offset Limited

13 14 15 16 17 10 9 8 7 6 5 4 3 2 1

Osprey Publishing is supporting the Woodland Trust, the UK's leading woodland conservation charity, by funding the dedication of trees.

www.ospreypublishing.com

CONTENTS

EARLY YEARS

From the very beginning, the Fairchild Republic A-10 Thunderbolt II was built to fight the tough fight. Down low, taking and giving punishment, was where the A-10 would earn its reputation. With its design being heavily influenced by the USAF's experiences in Vietnam, the A-10 was created to fight the next 'big war' that most believed would start in the Fulda Gap, in West Germany, when the armies of the Warsaw Pact rolled westward. Here, the A-10 would face the very best the Soviet Union could throw at it in terms of surface-to-air weaponry (both guided and unguided), and the aircraft was expected to leave a trail of destroyed Communist armour in its wake.

Although the A-10 may have been named in deference to another Republic aircraft, the P-47 of World War 2 fame, the Thunderbolt II name is seldom seen and less often heard spoken. Rather, Republic had a history of giving unofficial names to its aircraft that involved the use of the word 'hog'. The straight-winged F-84 was given the nickname of 'Groundhog', the swept-wing F-84F became 'Superhog' and the F-105 was the 'Ultra-Hog'. Given the A-10's rugged design features and ungainly lines, especially when compared to other aircraft performing the close air support (CAS) mission, the name 'Warthog' was affectionately bestowed upon the A-10. The newest Republic 'Hog' was born.

Beginning life as the Attack Experimental (AX) programme for the US Air Force (USAF) in June 1966, the AX was to be an aircraft that would be able to absorb battle damage, offer superior low-speed handling and carry a large amount of ordnance while performing the CAS mission. With the war in Vietnam still raging, the goal of the AX was to produce an aircraft that could support troops on the ground, effect search and rescue (SAR) missions and possess the ability to interdict the Ho Chi Minh trail and return home to fly again. However, as American involvement lessened in Vietnam, the focus of the AX was redirected to Europe and the Soviet Union's three-to-one battle tank superiority. The AX programme was duly repackaged as a solution to NATO's numerical inferiority.

Less than a year later, in March 1967, 21 companies were issued with a request for proposal (RFP) for the AX, and by August 1970 six companies had responded with designs aimed at fulfilling the requirement. Initial estimates from the USAF were for 600 aircraft at $1.4 million dollars each. In the competition to build the AX, two companies – Northrop and Fairchild Republic – were selected to build two prototypes each on

Carrying dummy AGM-65 Maverick missiles, the first YA-10A prototype (71-1369) is seen on a test flight from Edwards AFB during the aircraft's evaluation phase. This jet would fly for nearly three years, and accumulate just under 600 flight hours, before being retired *(USAF)*

Photographed on 26 January 1978, YA-10A 73-1669 takes on fuel behind a KC-135A in the airspace near Eielson AFB, Alaska. Wearing Arctic Red markings, 73-1669 was the last pre-production airframe to be built. Six months later, on 8 June, this aircraft was lost when both engines flamed out during the testing of a new gun propellant. The pilot was able to successfully eject *(USAF)*

18 December 1970. In March of the following year the aircraft had received their official designation, with Northrop's design becoming the YA-9 and Fairchild Republic's aircraft the YA-10. First flights for each type would occur in May 1972, and the fly-off was scheduled to commence five months later in the high desert of California at Edwards AFB.

For nearly two months the YA-9 and YA-10 flew against each other, with each aircraft accumulating more than 300 flying hours each during the evaluation. By 9 December 1972 the assessment was over. Five weeks later, on 18 January 1973, the Fairchild Republic YA-10 was declared the winner, based on several factors including access to underwing hardpoints, the ability to move swiftly from pre-production aircraft to production aircraft, the lower level of maintenance required and the selection of a pre-existing engine – the General Electric TF-34-100, a version of which was already in service with the US Navy's S-3A Viking. The USAF had a winning aircraft that was simple, survivable and lethal. Nevertheless, it was very much *unwanted* by senior officers in the post-Vietnam air force.

A huge advantage for the Fairchild Republic team was access to the library of empirical data collected by the company from examining combat damage and losses pertaining to the Republic F-105 Thunderchief during the Vietnam War. Engineers were able to study this information and break it down in such a way that they could work out how different systems were affected by flak damage. Information from fuel cell ruptures to hydraulic line failures to cockpit survivability was studied. This investment in the data at their disposal allowed the Fairchild Republic team to determine the best way to route flight controls, and also work out where redundancies would be needed.

Survivability attributes built into the YA-10 as a result included manual flight control revision, a titanium bathtub in which to enclose the pilot, a windscreen that could take a direct hit from a 23 mm projectile, redundancy between left and right rudders and elevators, and cable routing for the left and right hydraulic systems.

Yet despite the YA-10 winning the fly-off, this success alone was not sufficient enough to ensure the aircraft would enter production. A Congressional mandate required the USAF to hold a competition between the YA-10 and A-7D so as to measure the attributes of the new Fairchild Republic jet against the proposed A-7DER. For nearly a month in early

1974 the two airframes flew from McConnell AFB in Kansas. Following this 'second' fly-off the YA-10 again emerged the winner, thus allowing pre-production YA-10s to enter flight testing in 1975. A-10A 75-0258 subsequently became the first production aircraft to be turned over to the USAF, on 5 November 1975. Delivery of the first operational A-10 followed four months later, the 355th Tactical Fighter Wing (TFW) at Davis-Monthan AFB, in Tucson, Arizona, being the first frontline operator of the aircraft.

When Fairchild Republic was designing the AX's offensive weaponry, it canvassed the opinion of a group of A-1 Skyraider pilots who had flown in Vietnam. The one thing they had all said they wanted in the A-1, but did not have, was a 'big gun'. The 'big gun' chosen for the YA-10 was the General Electric GAU-8 Avenger 30 mm cannon. The GAU-8 has seven barrels that allow for a high rate-of-fire, originally available in a low mode of 2100 rounds per minute (rpm) or a high setting of 4200 rpm. Eventually, the rate-of-fire would be set at 3900 rpm. The GAU-8 system is enormous, weighing in at more than 4000 lbs when paired with a full magazine of ammunition. The gun can fire either PGU-13 high explosive incendiary (HEI) or PGU-14 armour-piercing incendiary (API) rounds, the latter containing a depleted uranium projectile to penetrate tank armour.

While the GAU-8 is the main weapon for the A-10, the 'Hog' has 11 weapons hardpoints from which to hang ordnance. Offensively, the A-10 can carry a wide variety of weaponry, including dumb bombs ranging up to 2000 lbs in size, either electro-optical (EO) or imaging infrared (IIR) guided AGM-65D Maverick missiles and

YA-10A 71-1369 was attached to a three-axis pedestal at the Rome Air Development Center's Newport Test Site during positioning system tests for the jet's various navigation antennae. The A-10's myriad stores pylons are clearly visible from this unusual angle *(USAF)*

The size of the General Electric GAU-8/A Avenger 30 mm cannon is clearly revealed in this famous publicity photograph from the early 1970s. The gun system weighs 4029 lbs (1828 kg) when carrying a maximum ammunition load. Measuring 19 ft 5.5 in (5.931 m) from the muzzle to the rear of the ammunition system, the GAU-8 requires power from two 77 hp electric motors for it to fire *(USAF)*

A-10A 78-0652, assigned to the 174th TFW of the New York ANG, is seen between sorties during exercise *Sentry Castle 81*. 'The Boys from Syracuse' were instrumental in getting the A-10 the improvements it needed in the form of the LASTE upgrade. The 174th FW flew the A-10 for almost a decade from 1979 to 1988 *(USAF)*

various cluster munitions and rockets, including White Phosphorus (WP) in LAU-131 pods, which can be used in the Forward Air Controller (Airborne) (FAC(A)) mission. While offensive armament is the A-10's reason for being, the 'Hog' is capable of defending itself via AIM-9 Sidewinder heat-seeking air-to-air missiles, an ECM pod and ALE-40 chaff and flare dispensers.

The first major upgrade for the A-10 arrived too late for use in Operation *Desert Storm* in early 1991. The low-altitude safety and targeting enhancement (LASTE) system was the first 'high tech' equipment that the A-10 would receive. LASTE was brought into service through the lobbying efforts of Air National Guard (ANG) and Air Force Reserve (AFRes) squadrons, who stressed the need for a computer in the aeroplane to facilitate the fitment of a ground collision avoidance system due to a number of airframes being lost during low-level training. Among the pilots, the ulterior motive for getting the computer was its ability to constantly compute impact points for the bombs and bullets they expended. The 138th Tactical Fighter Squadron (TFS) of the New York ANG drove the implementation of the LASTE programme.

LASTE also gave the aircraft an autopilot feature and improved cockpit lighting that allowed the introduction of night-vision goggles. External IR lighting was added to the A-10 at this time too. It would be almost a decade until a targeting pod was made available to the jet, however, with ANG and AFRes units again spearheading the requirement on the eve of Operation *Iraqi Freedom* (OIF).

Ironically, the toughest engagements the A-10 would have to fight would be for its very survival in USAF service, these 'clashes' taking place far from any battlefield. Indeed, this campaign would be fought in the corridors of the Pentagon, the halls of Congress and within communities surrounding A-10 bases across the Continental US. An aeroplane the USAF never wanted but chose to accept simply to keep the US Army out of the fixed wing aircraft business, and thus deny it a slice of Air Force funding, the A-10 has always been the unwanted child of America's youngest military branch. Loved by the pilots that fly it and the troops on the ground that it has spent almost four decades protecting, the A-10 has always been able to finish a fight, either over Iraq, Bosnia, Afghanistan, Libya or inside the offices of Washington, D.C.

OPERATION

ANACONDA

For nearly 17 minutes on the morning of 11 September 2001 there was great uncertainty about what had happened in New York City. Had the aircraft that had crashed into the North Tower of the World Trade Center been involved in a terrible accident, or was this a deliberate act of terror? At 0903 hrs, when United Airlines Flight 175 crashed into the South Tower, all ambiguity was removed. There was no longer any doubt that the United States had been attacked, and almost immediately the blame for the hijackings that day was pinned on Osama bin Laden and his al-Qaeda terrorist organisation. Attention turned toward Afghanistan, where the terrorist leader and most of his followers operated from. There was little doubt that an American military response would soon follow, but how and when were not immediately clear.

Halfway across the world at Osan AB, in South Korea, Capt Scott Campbell had just returned to his dorm, his work day complete. For Capt Campbell it was just after 2100 hrs as he turned on the 'morning' news from home. He was a recent Weapons School graduate and had been at Osan for almost nine months. Assigned to the 25th FS 'Assam Draggins', where he was the weapons and tactics officer, Capt Campbell was to spend a year flying A-10s on the Korean peninsula. He recalled;

'I turned on the TV and the first aeroplane had already hit the "twin towers". I was watching it live, listening to the commentary, as nobody knew what was going on yet. There was talk about an aeroplane that may have gone off course and crashed. That was when the United Airlines aeroplane hit the second tower.

'I picked up the phone and called Capt Clarence Johnson, who had just left the squadron with me. I said "Dude, are you watching this?" Then the Pentagon was hit – Clarence's dad was serving there as a full colonel. Obviously something was terribly wrong, and we rushed back to the squadron just as they started recalling everyone. We started pulling A-10s off the ramp and closing them up in the HASs (hardened aircraft shelters).

'One of the weirdest things I recall seeing during this period was waking up on the morning of 12 September and seeing half of the Patriot missile batteries at Osan pointing south – they usually always point north. What in the world would ever cause us to point those Patriots south? The whole world was worried what was going to happen next. Who knew what the threat was at the time? The only thing we knew for sure was that as A-10 pilots, we were going nowhere. Korea was absolutely the last place you wanted to be as an A-10 pilot because the jets were never going to be moved off the peninsula. We were sure that we were going to miss out on this war.'

The A-10 has always been about the gun – the aeroplane was built around the GAU-8/A Avenger after all. Firing at a fixed rate of 3900 rounds per minute – although typically fired only in two- or three-second bursts – the 30 mm rounds exit the barrel at an astonishing speed of 3240 ft per second *(Gary Wetzel)*

OEF BEGINS

Operation *Enduring Freedom* (OEF) began on 7 October 2001 as the US forces launched air strikes and fired Tomahawk missiles from ships and submarines (as did submarines of the Royal Navy) at Taleban and al-Qaeda positions throughout Afghanistan. A total of 31 targets were struck that first night, and over the next two months land-based USAF and carrier-based US Navy aircraft would fly almost 6500 combat missions. Although Naval Aviators would fly more than 70 per cent of the sorties due to the paucity of bases surrounding land-locked Afghanistan, USAF aircraft would employ almost 70 per cent of the nearly 18,500 weapons expended in support of OEF in the first eight weeks of the campaign.

The initial goal of the American military effort was to disrupt al-Qaeda's ability to function as a cohesive organisation, applying pressure to disrupt any attempts at further terrorist actions and generally keeping the enemy on the move. Additionally, the destruction of Taleban forces and supporting infrastructure would deny surviving al-Qaeda members the sanctuary offered to them by their host nation's controlling regime. Special Forces (SOF) teams would be the first American military personnel to land in Afghanistan, joining forces with the Northern Alliance to disrupt and destroy Taleban and al-Qaeda strongholds through the use of judicious and sustained air strikes.

The latter were flown in the main by USAF B-1, B-2 and B-52 bombers, F-15E Strike Eagles, F-16 Vipers and US Navy F-14 Tomcats and F/A-18 Hornets. The A-10 was not in this inventory of participants, instead standing Combat Search and Rescue (CSAR) alert at Ahmed Al Jaber AB, in Kuwait, and flying Operation *Southern Watch* (OSW) missions over southern Iraq as part of the 332nd Air Expeditionary Group (AEG). The primary reason why A-10s were not involved in the initial phase of OEF was the 'drive time' from Al Jaber to the skies of Afghanistan. The co-located Strike Eagles and Vipers could make the trip in three hours, while the appreciably slower 'Hog' would take more than five hours. Furthermore, OEF was initially 'SOF centric'. This essentially meant that most missions took the form of ground-directed interdiction (GDI) strikes, where SOF teams identified targets from the ground and directed interdiction from the air.

Having said that, the A-10 came close to making its OEF debut in mid-October 2001 during Operation *Rhino*. Launched on the 20th of the month, it involved the airborne insertion of 199 US Army Rangers from the 3rd Battalion, 75th Ranger Regiment. Preceded by a B-2 strike and protected by an orbiting AC-130 gunship, the Rangers parachuted from four MC-130 *Combat Talon* transports and seized an airstrip near Kandahar. They immediately assessed its viability in support of future air operations.

Lt Col Matt Neuenswander was deputy commander of the 332nd AEG at this time, and explained how the group was notified about *Rhino*;

'On the night of 9 October the 332nd AEG was informed of the upcoming mission. The A-10s at Al Jaber at that point were from the Maryland ANG's 104th FS, and we had been asked to provide some "Hogs" for CAS for the operation. The initial plan was to launch the A-10s from Jaber, fly the mission and recover them in Jacobabad, Pakistan. However, diplomatic clearance could not be secured and the recovery site for the A-10s was shifted to Seeb, Oman. The Baltimore [104th FS] guys did a tremendous amount of work – which would turn out to be fortuitous months later – devising routes, creating refuelling packages, locating divert bases and noting runway information at these locations. We had planned for 12-hour OEF sorties for the A-10s.

'On the evening of the 17th I was on a C-130 with its engines running, preparing to fly to Seeb, when the A-10 portion of the mission was cancelled as Oman would not grant the clearance we needed. I put all of the flight planning in a briefcase and kept it behind my desk in the operations centre, thinking that if they have to do something later with the A-10s, this would be handy.'

Almost six months later Lt Col Neuenswander would find himself reaching for those plans.

THE SHAH-I-KOT

Operation *Anaconda* was born in the shadows of the battle for the Tora Bora region of the central eastern border area of Afghanistan, and the mistakes that happened there. Several months had passed since the five-day battle in December 2001, and during this time intelligence reports had begun to indicate that a large number of Taleban and al-Qaeda fighters were spending the winter months in an eastern Afghan valley, preparing to emerge during the spring to fight again. The target of Operation *Anaconda* would be the Shah-i-Kot Valley. For the first time a significant number of conventional forces would be joining SOF teams as part of *Anaconda*.

Fighting alongside Afghan National Forces, the American troops had a clear objective – catch the enemy in the villages surrounding the valley and prevent any of them from escaping safely into Pakistan, as happened during the battle for Tora Bora.

Control of the planning for *Anaconda* was passed to Combined Joint Task Force (TF) Mountain in early February. This organisation was lead by the headquarters element of the 10th Mountain Division, which, prior to this, had been assigned security operations in Uzbekistan and Kandahar, and had not deployed to Afghanistan as a full division.

Requests to bring in components to set up and maintain an air support operations centre (ASOC) that would have been in radio range of the Shah-i-Kot Valley were rejected, and this denial of forces would eventually produce near disastrous consequences.

An ASOC is the nerve centre of the theatre air control system/army air-ground system (TACS/AAGS). Traditionally, CAS requests are generated by the enlisted terminal air controller (ETAC) in the frontline and then passed up through battalion, brigade and division levels until they reach the ASOC, which then coordinates and directs CAS missions. The lack of this formalised structure controlling air assets during *Anaconda* would nearly prove catastrophic.

Initially, the USAF was kept out of the planning for *Anaconda*, and it was only dealt into the operation a week before the launch date. Lt Gen Michael Moseley, the Combined Forces Air Component Commander (CFACC), was alerted by his subordinates to an upcoming operation while on a trip outside the region. Furthermore, the Combined Air Operations Center (CAOC) at Prince Sultan Air Base in Saudi Arabia, which was the overall authority for air operations in this theatre, had not been involved in *Anaconda* prior to the end of February. Even staff officers from a US Navy carrier battle group that positioned in the Northern Arabian Sea to support the operation was searching for more information about it, specifically exactly where *Anaconda* was going to take place!

The 332nd AEG was to provide a large portion of the air power to *Anaconda*, yet the group was not exposed to the battle plan until four days prior, as Lt Col Neuenswander explained;

'Col Dave Nichols, the commander of the 332nd AEG, and I were notified on 27 February that *Anaconda* was going to happen. We got the 100+ page PowerPoint presentation and we looked it over. Col Nichols told me to call the CAOC back and ask what they needed us to do, and what our tasking was going to be. They told us they wanted two 24/7 two-ship CAS CAPs during *Anaconda*. The 332nd was not going to be responsible for manning them all the time, however.

'Following a further discussion with Col Nichols, I got back with the CAOC and had a discussion with them about whether they had enough command and control up there. I told them that I didn't think they did, but their response was they had enough for the two two-ships being committed to the operation. In that respect they were right, and I told them so, but I also told them that if the operation "went south" they didn't. Up to this point there had been a number of named operations that had not amounted to much, and as a group [which controlled F-15Es and F-16s, as well as A-10s], the 332nd had not dropped a bomb since 18 December. This led the CAOC to believe that they had what they needed going into *Anaconda*.'

On 2 March TF Mountain launched Operation *Anaconda*. Helicopters inserted troops into blocking positions, and almost immediately they came under heavy fire from an enemy that was not waiting out the winter in the villages as expected, but firmly entrenched atop the peaks and mountains. Without organic firepower in the form of artillery and heavy mortars, the troops of TF Mountain were now dependent on the presence of five AH-64A Apaches and the other air power overhead. The battlefield helicopters saved the lives of many TF Mountain soldiers that morning, and may have saved the operation. However, there were not enough of them, and of those five helicopters only two were able to return to the fight following severe battle damage.

'I was in the expeditionary operations centre on the morning of 2 March', Lt Col Neuenswander recalled, 'and you could tell listening to the SATCOM that the operation was going bad almost immediately. With Col Nichols in crew rest, I called our squadron commanders in and told them they needed to put more pilots in crew rest because I had a feeling things were going to change. And I was right. By that evening the CAOC was talking about a "max effort" the next day, even cancelling the OSW sorties'.

3 March proved to be a long day for Lt Col Neuenswander. The 332nd AEG had been launching F-16s and F-15Es in support of *Anaconda*, with most OSW sorties having been cancelled following the hasty shift in mission focus to Afghanistan. Aircrew returning from OEF were all reporting that the situation in the Shah-i-Kot Valley was a mess, with virtually no command and control (C2) overhead. Aircraft would arrive on station and then circle for hours waiting to deliver ordnance, only to depart the valley when they ran low on fuel and then have to return to Al Jaber with all their bombs still aboard. More C2 was needed, but there was no agreement on how it was to be implemented. The absence of the EC-130E Airborne Battlefield Command and Control Center (ABCCC) in particular produced a profoundly negative effect on the combat missions. With no ASOC in place to support *Anaconda*, there was a desperate need for control as far as the air effort was concerned.

Controllers aboard AWACS assets in-theatre were not trained to sort out troops in contact (TIC) calls and requests for CAS – moving aircraft in and out of the battle space and coordinating tankers was where their training and mission was focused. Another C2 aircraft in the form of an E-8 JSTARS was hastily pushed into the fight to help mitigate the growing problems on the ground. The JSTARS' crew was augmented by SOF personnel and F-16 pilots from the South Carolina ANG. Although the E-8 was not a perfect fit for *Anaconda*, it was a step in the right direction.

Exhausted, Lt Col Neuenswander left the expeditionary operations centre at around 1900 hrs on 3 March;

'I headed out to get some dinner and then to get some sleep. At about 2000 hrs I got back to my room, and I had just got out of my clothes and was about to go to bed when the phone rang. It was the ops centre. I was told to get back over there as we were now going to take the A-10s forward. By the time I got back there Col Nichols had just finished debriefing his OEF flight. He had then taken a call from deputy CFACC, Rear Adm David Nichols, who wanted us to take the A-10s forward following news that the Apaches had been badly shot up. TF Mountain urgently needed CAS aircraft in-theatre.

A 500-lb Mk 82 airburst bomb affixed to an A-10A of the 74th EFS at Bagram in November 2006. The unguided Mk 82 has been the main bomb carried by A-10As in OEF since Operation *Anaconda*. With a risk estimate distance of 300 m, the airburst Mk 82 is the near perfect weapon for the 'soft' targets that proliferate in OEF *(Capt Tom Harney)*

Forward-firing weapons such as the White Phosphorous (WP) rockets being fired from an LAU-131 pod in this photograph, Maverick missiles and the gun have been favoured by 'Hog' pilots since the aeroplane first entered service. The ability to fire rockets has allowed the A-10 to perform the FAC(A) role for other 'Hogs' or Coalition strike aircraft *(Gary Wetzel)*

'I called Lt Col Arden Dahl, CO of the 74th Expeditionary Fighter Squadron [EFS], and told him to grab his operations officer and come and see me as it looked like we were taking the A-10s forward. *All* the "Hog" pilots came over to the mission planning cell [MPC], and I told them to get out of there because some of them needed to be in crew rest as they would be flying the following morning. Immediately, we began to plan the next day's mission.'

Capt Scott Campbell, who had formerly flown A-10s from Osan AB, was one of the few 'Hog' pilots who did not immediately head to the operations centre to find out when he would be flying in support of *Anaconda*, and whether he would be involved in one of the first missions. Instead, he was in the gym working out when a squadronmate from the 74th came in and told him to head directly to the MPC. 'Up to this point', recalled Capt Campbell, 'it had strictly been a Viper and Strike Eagle show, and us A-10 guys had been told that "OEF was not for us, and never would be, so we should stop drooling about it – you are not going". Well, when I walked into the MPC Col Nichols and Lt Cols Neuenswander and Dahl were all there, deep in discussion. I had a feeling that I was finally going to get my wish. As soon as I walked in I was told I was in crew rest, and that I would be flying in a two-ship with Lt Col Ed Kostelnik as my wingman.

'Before I left the MPC I was able to talk to Maj Robert Hetland, the 332nd's weapons officer. He and I discussed shifting the standard conventional load (SCL) from OSW to OEF, and doing it all in a 12-hour window. For OSW, the SCL was for killing armour, which meant that the jets carried CBU-87s, IIR AGM-65D Mavericks, rockets, an ECM pod, an AIM-9 missile and the gun loaded with a combat mix – our anti-armour mix of five depleted uranium (DU) rounds for every API round. The new target sets in Afghanistan were dismounted troops and technical vehicles – soft targets in air-to-ground parlance – so we didn't need the anti-armour SCL.

'We decided to swap the CBUs for Mk 82 500-lb bombs with airburst fuses, as the latter was going to maximise the kill radius against flesh and soft targets. We definitely wanted white WP rockets, so we elected to load three pods worth because it sounded like we were going to be doing CAS. We also loaded some IR flares – LUU-19s – and elected to keep our Mavericks, using the weapons' IIR as a poor man's FLIR. That was how we found targets at night in the A-model. Then we changed the ammunition, replacing all the DU and API shells with a full load of high explosive [HE] rounds. We dropped the ECM pod and the AIM-9s as well. The first combat load for OEF was four Mk 82 airburst bombs, two IIR Mavericks, one SUU-25 canister containing LUU-19s, three rocket pods and HEI for the gun.

'I left the MPC to find Lt Col Kostelnik and tell him what was happening. At first he didn't believe me, but I finally convinced him that I was not messing with him. I was excited, but at the same time I was trying to lower my expectations, as both he and I expected that the whole thing would be called off the following morning.'

Mission planning continued throughout the night at the MPC. The hard part was not launching A-10s to support *Anaconda* but meeting the requirements established by the CAOC for the air coverage they were to provide once in-theatre. To fulfil the demands being placed on the 332nd it would be necessary to stage the A-10s from somewhere other than Al Jaber, where the flight time to Afghanistan was five hours. The CAOC quickly supplied a list of potential sites from which an expeditionary group could operate. The choices included Seeb in Oman, Karshi-Kanabad in Uzbekistan, Kandahar in Afghanistan and Jacobabad in Pakistan.

'We reached in and pulled out those plans from October and decided to start with them', explained Lt Col Neuenswander. 'We had to figure out how we were going to get to the new base, how we were going to build an expeditionary bomb dump there and what logistical support was required in order to move the maintenance personnel in a single day. We also needed four days' worth of munitions in order to commence operations.

'Once we started looking at the possible locations we might fly from, it quickly became clear that Jacobabad was the one that best fitted the operating environment we required. I called the CAOC and told them that operating from Pakistan was the only option available that met their established criteria for the A-10. By the next morning [4 March] none of the locations offered to us had been approved. Nevertheless, the CAOC elected to launch the first pair of A-10s from Al Jaber, despite not knowing where they were going to land them!'

By the time the first A-10s took off from Al Jaber to support *Anaconda*, things had gone from bad to worse in the Shah-i-Kot Valley. Desperate to increase the number of observation posts in the southern portion of the valley, TF Mountain had made the decision to insert two additional SEAL teams to aid with surveillance and the calling in of air strikes on al-Qaeda and Taleban forces fighting in the valley.

The dominant feature of the Shah-i-Kot Valley was the 10,000-ft peak of Takur Ghar. Imagery indicated the peak was clear of enemy forces when the SEAL team ('Mako 30') departed Bagram in a MH-47 belonging to the 160th Special Operations Aviation Regiment. With the original insertion point 1300 m east of the peak of Takur Ghar no longer available due to numerous technical delays that had prevented the landing of the team, the only way the SEALs would reach the peak before daylight was if they were inserted directly onto it.

At 0248 hrs on 4 March – almost three hours after the SEALs had boarded their first MH-47 – the Chinook approached the peak of Takur Ghar, only for the crew to discover that the peak was anything but empty. Fresh footprints in the snow, an unmanned DShk 12.7 mm heavy machine gun and other signs of a significant enemy presence sparked an internal debate about proceeding with the landing. Almost instantly the Chinook began taking RPG and small arms fire. Three RPG impacts disabled the helicopter's right turbine, causing the loss of one engine and electrical and hydraulic power. As the MH-47 struggled to remain airborne and depart the Hot Landing Zone, SEAL ABN1 Neil Roberts, who was preparing to exit the aircraft, slipped and fell from the Chinook as it drifted away from the peak. The damaged helicopter struggled on for four miles before crash-landing in the valley.

Determined to return to the peak and attempt a rescue of their team member, the SEALs boarded another MH-47 and headed back to Takur Ghar. At 0455 hrs the second Chinook landed on the peak and was met by significant ground fire. This time, however, the remaining members of 'Mako 30' were able to exit the helicopter in the hope of rescuing ABN1 Roberts. In the ensuing firefight one member of the team, an Air Force combat controller, was killed by enemy fire and several SEALs were wounded. Understanding the hopelessness of their situation, the team leader ordered his men to disengage and commence an arduous descent from the peak. He also requested that the Ranger Quick Reaction Force (QRF) at Bagram be scrambled to come to their rescue.

The QRF was duly launched, but following a series of communication errors and a total misunderstanding of where 'Mako 30' currently was, the Rangers were instructed to land at the peak of Takur Ghar. At approximately 0610 hrs, the third Chinook to approach the peak that night was also met with significant ground fire, forcing the helicopter to crash-land near the mountain summit. The battle of Roberts' Ridge was now fully engaged, and by the time it was over seven of the eight Americans killed during *Anaconda* would have fallen on Takur Ghar. The QRF was pinned down in a struggle for survival and the CAS effort was running at 'full throttle', yet the premier CAS aircraft in the USAF inventory had yet to make its entry into the fight. That would soon change, however, as the first A-10s were now just hours away from departing Al Jaber for Afghanistan.

Whilst walking out to his A-10 with Lt Col Kostelnik on the morning of 4 March, Capt Campbell definitely had his doubts about how the day was going to turn out. His concerns were warranted when the 'smart pack' he was handed en route to the jet contained Russian maps of Afghanistan, with cities, towns and geographic references in Cyrillic!

'The MPC had spent the entire night making maps and putting together this "smart pack" for us', explained Capt Campbell. 'We did not have maps of Afghanistan, and I was flying an A-10A that lacked mapping radar, so I needed maps. There was a lot of confusion coming from the Army about the state of the *Anaconda* battlefield. MPC got this printout from the CAOC of the airspace coordination order (ACO). It told us where the restricted fire and no fire areas were. We could take that information and plug it into Falcon View [a Windows-based mapping application created by the Georgia Tech Research Institute that displays various types of maps and geographically referenced overlays] and it would produce a printed map featuring little circles that indicated the exact location of the restricted areas.

'I was handed a map of this five-kilometre by nine-kilometre chunk of battlespace that had circles all over it! I was expecting some sort of briefing on where the friendlies were. Once we finally got overhead the troops in contact I might as well have shredded the map as it was useless. By the time it was printed out, we briefed, stepped to the jet and then took a five-hour flight to Afghanistan, the information on the map was almost 12 hours old.'

However, the biggest problem facing the two A-10 pilots was where they were going to land once they had finished providing CAS over the Shah-i-Kot. Capt Campbell was provided with approach plates and airport diagrams for several possible landing sites. Aside from the rudimentary maps and possible landing information, the 'smart pack', which was nearly three inches thick, outlined operational procedures to be followed once in-theatre. It also contained the different frequencies the A-10 pilots would need to communicate with AWACS, JSTARs, ETACs on the ground and air traffic controllers at the various airports that could provide potential shelter to the 'Hog' pilots at mission end.

'I was stoked, but I just felt completely clueless walking out the door', Capt Campbell recalled as he approached his A-10 on the flightline at Al Jaber. 'The thing that calmed me down was when a couple of my squadronmates said "You've got five hours drive time. Yeah you will be on the tanker a couple of times, but you have five hours to figure everything out". They were right. During the drive over, Lt Col Kostelnik and I started going through the "smart packs", flipping from page to page and comparing notes on how we thought it was going to look. Still, there was nothing, I repeat nothing, that could have prepared us for what the reality of the situation would really be like'.

With the two A-10s now in the air, Lt Col Neuenswander left the MPC at 0900 hrs (1130 OEF time). Nearly two days without sleep was beginning to take its toll, and he made his way back to his room and went to bed. He would get just 30 minutes rest before being summoned back to the MPC, as a forward operating location had been negotiated for the A-10s tasked with supporting *Anaconda*. It was going to be Jacobabad.

A key factor in allowing American fighter aircraft to operate from within Pakistan was that CFACC Gen Moseley had had a war college classmate who was a ranking official in the Pakistani defence hierarchy. As long as the Americans were in contact with the enemy in the Shah-i-Kot, the A-10s could stay in Pakistan, but once the major fighting was over they would have to return to Kuwait. At 1230 hrs Lt Col Neuenswander called the CAOC and informed them that the HC-130 crew sitting CSAR alert at Al Jaber was coming off alert, and it would be delivering the first personnel to support combat operations from Pakistan. The HC-130 would roll down the runway at Al Jaber at 1530 hrs on 4 March.

The initial A-10 mission to OEF was almost a false start, as the tanker for first in-flight refuelling arrived late. The two 'Hogs' had picked up a tailwind shortly after takeoff, and they arrived early in the refuelling track. Unable to talk to anyone due to their ultra high-frequency radios lacking any kind of signal, and the A-10A possessing no SATCOM capability, Capt Campbell and Lt Col Kostelnik simply 'hung on the fans' until the Bahrain-based tanker showed up and began dragging them towards Afghanistan.

After five-and-a-half hours, Capt Campbell and Lt Col Kostelnik arrived over the Shah-i-Kot Valley, and it was close to sunset. There would be almost no chance to see the valley in daylight. As the A-10 pilots looked down at the rapidly darkening landscape, they realised that the problems they would face trying to pick friend from foe on the ground had just gotten far worse.

'I was originally hoping that we would get there in time to have a look at the terrain in order to ascertain where our targets were', Capt Campbell recalled. 'We knew what it looked like on paper, but that is not the same as putting your "Mk 1 eyeball" on it. We didn't have the sensors for low-light operations in the A-10A. It was like looking into a black hole, knowing that you have high terrain on either side that further complicates things. We had to be higher than we would normally have been so as to stay away from those peaks – home to many of the AAA [anti-aircraft artillery] threats. The height at which these weapons were sited amplified their level of threat to us. We were forced to stay up around 20,000 ft. At this altitude, with ten of eleven hardpoints loaded with ordnance, the jet weighed almost 45,000 lbs, making it an absolute pig to fly.

'The sun had set, but there was still enough of a glow in the sky at our altitude to badly affect our NVGs. I could only look down with my goggles when I had the sun at my back, so I was forced to search the ground from west to east. When I came around in my orbit and tried to look from east to west, I had to pop my goggles up because I couldn't see a thing.

'To make things even more challenging, the comms were a mess. AWACS had nothing really to tell us, we didn't have an ASOC to talk to and there was nobody to give us an area of operations (AO) update, which as a CAS guy I would have expected. Nobody was on any of the frequencies we had been given. We went back to the AWACS and requested another "freq" to try. We had a sheet that probably had 100 "freqs" on it, but the list didn't have who was assigned to any of them – it just had lots of tactical air direction (TAD) numbers. We decided to try them all, so between the two of us we just flipped through the frequencies. I'd be on one "freq" trying to figure out who was operating on it while Lt Col Kostelnik spoke to the AWACS controller to let him know that we were up on this TAD, and asking who was on the other TAD.

ETACs were the vital link between ground forces and air power in OEF. Working the radios, firing weapons and remaining focused under fire were the norm for these highly trained individuals. When *Anaconda* began there were 37 ETACs in the Shah-i-Kot Valley *(USAF)*

'Eventually, we got onto a frequency where there were three different guys screaming for CAS. No one had priority, as there was no ASOC to determine who needed CAS ahead of who. I had to make that decision, working out who to support first. I started talking to the guy who was screaming the loudest – that was the best I could do.

'The ETAC I started talking to was screaming for emergency CAS [ECAS], and he was using an IR strobe to mark his position – a blinking light in my NVGs in the middle of a black abyss. His squad was taking mortar fire from about 700 m south of their position, and he needed the bad guys taken out as they were steadily walking the mortars in on them. This was all the information I was given about the location of my target. There was no 9-line briefing and no map coordinates. It was a "poor man's call for fire", and he was asking for our Mk 82 airburst bombs. I was more than a little worried about using them, however, as at the time we did not have a risk estimate distance for the airburst. We had an estimate for impact-fused Mk 82s, but not the airburst version. We knew the latter had a bigger blast diameter than a standard Mk 82, but we did not know just how much bigger.

'I had nothing to aim at but an IR strobe, and this guy was calling for me to rip down some airbursts! I was not comfortable just rolling in and dropping on what I thought was my target 700 m south of this IR marker. And I was still having a hard time seeing the marker with the sky glow – I could only see the marker during half of my orbit. We needed a unit of measure other than the strobe, so I prepared to fire a WP rocket at the target area. At least with the WP, unless I got excessively close, I was not going to kill anybody.

'I rolled in from the "high teens" with a two-mile slant range and pickled off the WP using a 30-45 HATR (high altitude tactical rocket) delivery. I was doing my best to try and figure out how far 700 m was from the strobe prior to firing the WP. Still unsure when I pickled off the rocket, I erred on the side of caution in my aim. I put the WP round into the middle of the black hole, after which the ETAC told me to move 300 m closer. To me it didn't matter what the actual distance was – I at least knew that in the ETAC's mind my WP rockets were only a klick [one kilometre] away. He was telling me that he wanted the bombs aimed a third of the distance from his strobe to where the WP had hit the ground. And that is where I told Lt Col Kostelnik to drop his weapons after I came off my diving WP delivery. It was going to take me about ten minutes to get back to altitude as I climbed away at 160 knots. Lt Col Kostelnik pickled two Mk 82s and the ETAC reported a direct hit. Contact had now completely ceased, and they were no longer taking mortar fire.

'As we were climbing back up into our orbit over the valley, "Spartan" (British AWACS) called to tell us that a B-52 strike was inbound with a TST [Time Sensitive Target] mission assigned by the CAOC. I raised the "Buff" – whose call sign was "Cujo" – on the radio and got him to pass us his target, run-in heading and angels. He was ten minutes out, ready to lay down a string of 2000-lb JDAMs [Joint Direct Attack Munitions]. Lt Col Kostelnik and I plotted out his run with grease pencils onto our maps. The "Buff's" target was one klick south of the troops we had just been supporting, and his bomb fall line was going to run right through the orbit of an AC-130 gunship that was flying beneath us – I didn't think the Spectre's crew would be too happy with that! I immediately called the bomber off, gave him a new run-in heading and moved the gunship south so that the "Buff" was clear to make the strike. After that we needed gas.'

With their first vul period having ended, the two A-10 pilots headed out to the tanker track to refuel. Although no longer searching in the near dark for targets, their night was not about to get any easier conducting a seemingly routine aerial refuelling operation. With the surface-to-air threat not yet fully understood in OEF, the tanker tracks in Afghanistan were all above 24,000 ft. This meant that refuelling a fully loaded A-10 became rather a complicated affair. At that altitude and with all the ordnance being carried by the jet, its TF34-GE-100A engines would be 'parked at max' throughout the refuelling cycle. The tanker would also have to fly as slowly as it could, the crew extending the jet's flaps so as to avoid it stalling.

The tanker also produced a huge bow wave that required a little bit of extra power from the receiver aircraft in order to get through it to the boom. However, already 'maxed out' on power, the A-10 would end up just sitting there behind the tanker, having run into the bow wave without any power spare to push through it in order to reach the probe. The only option available to the 'Hog' pilot at this point was to 'toboggan'. In A-10 jargon, 'tobogganing' meant that the tanker would enter a shallow dive, with the 'Hog' chasing it. With the tanker maintaining its airspeed, the simple principle of gravity would produce the necessary energy to allow the A-10 to push through the bow wave, connect with the probe and refuel.

Having used 'tobogganing' to top off their tanks, Capt Campbell and Lt Col Kostelnik headed back to the valley for their second vul period without knowing where they would be landing that night. The one thing they did know was that there was very little command and control in place in the skies over the *Anaconda* battlefield. AWACS controllers were working aircraft in and out of the area, and giving them safe altitudes for those movements, but they were unable to cope with the workload suddenly thrust upon them in a CAS-intensive environment. Previously in OEF, AWACS and CAS had been a much simpler affair, with a small group of SOF teams requesting support and AWACS passing on that information to the available, orbiting aircraft. Now, 37 different ETACs were in the Shah-i-Kot Valley and dozens of aircraft – US Navy and USAF – were being committed to the fight.

Preventing a mid-air collision was paramount, and a week later Capt Campbell would find out just how close he had come to being involved in such an accident during his first mission over the valley on the evening of 4 March. As he was completing one of his early passes overhead the ETAC he was supporting, Campbell unwittingly flew within 300 ft of an orbiting AC-130, which he and his wingman were not aware of. The gunship had been orbiting beneath them. A friend of Capt Campbell's who happened to be aboard the gunship described how the flightdeck crew could see the entire planform view of his A-10 'as big as Dallas' in front of them.

That night, the AC-130 was not the only thing that nearly collided with Capt Campbell. Unsure of the threat from AAA, the two A-10 pilots were using procedural deconfliction. This meant that their jets were totally blacked out, including their Night Vision Imaging System (NVIS) IR lights, which can be seen through night vision equipment.

'We were working with a second set of ETACs', Capt Campbell explained, 'and that was when we saw a Hornet flash through our formation. A red rotating beacon means that it is a US Navy aeroplane, so once we saw that we turned on our NVIS. A short while later and I almost had a Predator bounce off my canopy too. We were both probably thinking that the altitude we were operating at was exclusively ours, as no one was providing deconfliction. Right after that, just as we were talking with another ETAC, a bomb went off beneath our aeroplanes within our orbit, meaning that somebody had dropped through us! We get on the radio and asked AWACS if anybody else was working in our area but not talking to us. They replied that "Skinner 71" – a flight of US Navy Hornets – was in the area, but that they did not have permission to drop. Obviously, the Naval Aviators didn't get the word.'

Deconfliction was the biggest problem facing aircrews during *Anaconda* as the valley was literally filled with aircraft operating on different frequencies, with TST missions on one frequency and CAS on another, and nobody talking to each other. Lt Col Kostelnik and Capt Campbell immediately tasked themselves with providing the deconfliction required before something bad happened. *Anaconda* had begun with an AC-130 firing on a friendly convoy, killing one American soldier and several Afghans, and further fratricide was unacceptable.

'So we began working the radios, flying split ops', recalled Capt Campbell. 'I set up Lt Col Kostelnik as a tactical airborne coordinator aircraft (TAC-A), which was something we used to do back in the low altitude, Cold War days. We started to build a frequency plan whereby we had everyone on one "freq" when it came to checking in with us. That way we would know who they where, what they were flying and who they were working with. We had three radios in the jet, so we were simultaneously working a bunch of "freqs". The AWACS controllers were more than happy to hand off some of the workload. We spent our entire second vul period working the radios.'

Again needing fuel, the A-10s headed back to the tanker tracks for a top up. Whilst being refuelled Capt Campbell and Lt Col Kostelnik were informed that they would be landing at Jacobabad, but not until they had completed another vul period. CFACC was working through the carrier launch and recovery cycle in search of more strike assets (Tomcats and Hornets), and the CAOC wanted to ensure that it had enough air power stacked up over Afghanistan to support the operation. The A-10s headed back to the Shah-i-Kot Valley and began working with the JSTARS on station, call sign 'Stiletto'. It was tracking moving targets, and the A-10 pilots began the tedious process of attempting to identify the vehicles through a combination of NVGs and imaging from the seeker heads of the IIR Mavericks. It was taxing to say the least. A few vehicle convoys were chased but nothing could ever be positively identified before it was time for the A-10s to leave the valley for the last time and hit the last tanker for the night. Once refuelled, the pilots pointed the noses of their jets toward Jacobabad, 300 miles from the tanker track.

Despite the fact the A-10 pilots were now in the final phase of their lengthy mission, they still faced the considerable problem of getting local approval to land at a Pakastani air force base. 'About 100 miles out we tuned to the "freq" of the command post at Jacobabad and told them we were inbound, and to let our maintainers know', Capt Campbell explained. 'The response we got was "Who are you?" My first thought was "This is not going to go well". I was worried about the question, but at this point I knew they couldn't say no. We didn't have the fuel to turn around and go anywhere else, plus we had been airborne for almost 12 hours. We were landing, no matter what.

'I told them again who we were, instructed them to call the CAOC and told them that we were landing, so they needed to get ready for us. Still, I was hoping that it was all just a misunderstanding at local level, and that our guys were waiting for us on base. We lined up for the landing, and our instructions were to come in blacked out. Luckily I managed to get the jet down without stripping the landing gear off. Landing at night on goggles was something I had never done before – another first for me during that mission!

'When we taxied onto the small hammerhead at the end of the runway we could barely fit our jets in there, and sure enough there was no one around to meet us. I called the tower and asked where the de-arm crew was, and the response I got was "What's that?" Two Humvees armed with 0.50-cal machine guns came racing towards us. A number of soldiers armed with rifles jumped out of the vehicles once they had stopped, the troops setting up a defensive perimeter around our jets. I looked at Lt Col Kostelnik and said over the radio, "What is this place we've come to where we're in "dearm" and I have to have these guys defending us?!" Eventually, a maintainer from the USAF TF Dagger MH-53J detachment on base who had previously served as an A-10 crew chief some ten years earlier showed up. He had the basics on getting our unused ordnance safely pinned up.

'The idea was to hide us in F-16 revetments, but that was clearly not going to work. We shut the engines down and finished pinning the ordnance, after which a resourceful USAF staff sergeant found us cots, food and a shower. We then called back to Al Jaber and talked to Col Nichols, who told us that Lt Col Neuenswander and some others were on the way and would be arriving soon. He told us to get some rest, as we would be flying again the next day.'

After 11.5 hours in the air and seven aerial refuellings, the first A-10 mission of Operation *Anaconda* was over.

SUPPORT REACHES JACOBABAD

Arriving at Jacobabad at 0030 hrs on 5 March, the specially configured New York ANG HC-130 delivered Lt Cols Neuenswander and Robert Silva from the 74th EFS, along with a selection of pilots, maintainers and equipment. The ad-hoc command and control group was set up and running by about 0300 hrs. Having finally got some rest after arriving in Pakistan, Lt Col Neuenswander headed back to the new MPC to begin planning the next day's operations, which hopefully included the arrival of two more flights of A-10s. This would bring the total number of jets in-theatre to six as requested by the CAOC.

Conditions at Jacobabad were sparse in comparison with the 332nd's surroundings at Al Jaber, but fortunately for the group US SOF detachments that had been on base since OEF commenced had already established the essentials that were required. Tents provided shelter, there was a chow hall and the squadron's MPC was established in a run down hangar.

Capt Campbell and Lt Col Kostelnik awoke mid-morning on 5 March relieved to find that the promised HC-130 had indeed delivered some people they knew. 'It was nice when we got up the next morning and found Lt Cols Neuenswander and Silva at Jacobabad, as we could now plug back into the group matrix' Capt Campbell recalled. 'This meant that it was not completely "Capt Campbell making shit up as he went along". God knows where that would have taken us'.

Lt Col Neuenswander immediately waived the pilot rest requirement for Capt Campbell and Lt Col Kostelnik, and that afternoon the pair again headed into the Shah-i-Kot Valley. The previous night had seen near misses and problems with deconfliction of the airspace, especially with TST missions generated by the CAOC.

The agreement reached with Pakistan for the basing of A-10s at Jacobabad had hinged primarily on the local authorities being able to deny the presence of A-10s at the airfield. Thus, the 'Hogs' were meant to be hidden during daylight hours and only flown at night. However, it proved difficult to hide an aircraft as big as the A-10 in revetments designed for smaller F-16s – the wingspan of an A-10 is almost twice that of an F-16! *Anaconda* was not going well, and A-10s were needed over the valley both day and night. The decision from CFACC Lt Gen Moseley was to send the A-10s back to the Shah-i-Kot immediately (hence the launching of Capt Campbell and Lt Col Kostelnik), despite the agreement with Pakistan regarding daylight flight operations.

Capt Scott Campbell sits on the tanker in 74th EFS A-10A 79-0179 and takes on fuel for the second time on 5 March 2002. 'We were refuelling from a New Jersey ANG KC-135A, and the tanker guys all had friends or relatives who had been at the World Trade Center either working or as firemen or policemen, and they really wanted us to go get some of the enemy', recalled Capt Campbell. 'We left the tanker and went back into the Shah-i-Kot Valley, where we performed some target deconfliction for other strike aircraft, but nothing else. We went back to the tanker kind of bummed as we had wanted to return to them having expended all our weapons, and with tales to tell about how we had whacked a bunch of dudes. Well, a short while later, we did indeed drop our bombs, but we ended up with a different tanker for our fourth refuelling, so we never got to tell the New Jersey guys what we did' (Lt Col Scott Campbell)

Lt Col Ed Kostelnik drops away from the New Jersey ANG KC-135A whilst flying his first mission from Jacobabad on 5 March 2002. His jet is missing two 500-lb Mk 82 bombs from the outer stores pylons after he had dropped the pair the night before in the Shah-i-Kot Valley *(Lt Col Scott Campbell)*

The two A-10 pilots flew into Afghanistan after getting fuel from a New Jersey ANG KC-135A in the 'Bigfoot' air-to-air refuelling (AAR) track. Arriving over the valley, there was very little going on with the exception of some pre-planned targets being attacked by CAOC-controlled assets on the 'Whaleback' – the dominant feature within the Shah-i-Kot Valley. Capt Campbell and Lt Col Kostelnik spent their first vul period looking over the terrain with the 20 power binoculars they carried with them. They had not had a chance to do this the previous evening. With nothing going on, the pilots returned to the tanker for more fuel before heading back toward the Shah-i-Kot.

'We went back in for our last vul before we had to head home', said Capt Campbell. 'The sun was moving down as it was about 1600 hrs local. Having checked in, we were told to contact "Dragon 1-1" who was a 101st Airborne ETAC on one ridge north of Takur Ghar. He has been in working with a Predator that had picked up four vehicles moving through the southern end of the valley. The Predator had followed the vehicles into a valley south of "Dragon 1-1", and according to the reports the drone operator was seeing about 200-300 Taleban coming down the sides of the valley to meet up with the vehicles. The ETAC began pushing me a 9-line brief that included coordinates down to the tenths of minutes from information he was receiving from the Predator, as he had no eyes in the valley itself.

'To the south of him was "Jaguar 1-2", a USAF Special Tactics Squadron (STS) controller embedded with an Australian Army SAS team. He too couldn't see into the valley, but he was trying to help talk us on nevertheless. This valley was one of the "ratlines" the Army was worried about, the Taleban and al-Qaeda either reinforcing or escaping through it. This valley would eventually be named "EA Ratline", and it would become a free fire zone.

'I set up for my first pass to mark the valley entrance with a WP round, but came off dry as I was unsure if I had the right valley. Lt Col Kostelnik got on the radio and told me that he thought the ETAC was talking about the next valley to the south. He was right, so I rolled in and put two WP into the valley. Unfortunately, the valley was so deep that the smoke just hung there, and neither "Dragon" nor "Jaguar" could see my mark.

"Dragon" asked us to try again, and the rocket fired by Lt Col Kostelnik prompted the ETAC to confirm that this was indeed the right valley.

'As we climbed back up to altitude, I had "Popeye" flight – two US Navy Hornets – check in with me. I still had all four Mk 82s from the day before on my jet, and Lt Col Kostelnik also had two bombs remaining, as we hadn't rearmed before this mission. My intention was to start at the mouth of the valley and work west to east. I rolled in and "Dragon" gave me final clearance to drop. I put the four Mk 82s within a spacing of 75 ft right in the mouth of the valley. As I pulled off I rolled up and looked back to see a secondary explosion come up – I had hit the trucks. I told Lt Col Kostelnik to aim at the explosions, and he followed up with two more Mk 82s behind my four.

'Having delivered six bombs, we now cleared the area to allow the Hornets to come in from the west, where they had been orbiting, patiently waiting their turn to attack. Each Hornet was carrying two Mk 82 airbursts and two GBU-12 LGBs. They had all the target information they needed, as well as eyes on our bomb hits. I briefed them on the best run in to the target – west to east due to the time of day and setting sun, as well as the topography of the valley. Moments later they flew over the top of us, at which point I visually acquired them. I took final control of their attack, but left the abort authority with "Dragon 1-1". "Popeye 13" rolled in southwest to northeast in a diving delivery, but I did not see any impacts in the valley. "Popeye 14" rolled in next from the west over the top of me, and I saw only one good hit from the two bombs he dropped – they might have had a problem with their fuses. The Hornet pilots "bingo'd" out and headed home.

'We were running out of gas and really pushing it, but we knew there were enemy fighters trapped in the valley and we were just going to keep on pounding them. There really was no way out for them. We had yet to shoot the gun, and it was about time someone heard the weapon as there is nothing else that sounds like the A-10's cannon. I set up my attack run and rolled in, putting down two bursts totalling about 350 rounds of HEI. I shot from a 2.5-mile slant range at about 19,000 ft on a 45-degree wire. I pulled the trigger for the first burst for two seconds, before "walking" the gun further down the valley for another burst. Lt Col Kostelnik did exactly the same thing.

'Although we didn't have any BDA [battle damage assessment] on the target as we headed home, we knew that we had hit something. The blast from our six airburst Mk 82s would have been unbelievable in that confined space of the valley. "Jaguar 1-2" and the Aussie SAS team went up to the mouth of the valley the next day and reported a pink mist just hanging in the valley.

'"Spartan", the British AWACS, recognised that we had been in the target area longer than we should have, pushing past "bingo fuel" by a few hundred pounds. The controller offered to push the tanker towards us 30 nautical miles north of "Bigfoot" AAR and we graciously accepted.'

Five hours earlier, the second pair of A-10s bound for Jacobabad had left Al Jaber and were only now entering Afghanistan. The flight lead was Capt Andra Kniep, with Maj Dave Clinton on her wing. Following a quick handover brief from Capt Campbell, the A-10s pressed toward the Shah-i-Kot. The number of 'Hogs' supporting *Anaconda* had just doubled.

American forces survey 'EA Ratline' after *Anaconda* has ended. The vehicle seen in this photograph was just one of a number that were tracked into the area by an orbiting Predator. The steepness of the walls of the valley contributed to the effects of the weapons used during *Anaconda*, restricting the explosive power of the 500-lb Mk 82 airburst weapons, six of which were dropped by A-10s against the vehicles *(USAF)*

Another destroyed vehicle from 'EA Ratline', where Capt Campbell and Lt Col Kostelnik hit marshalling enemy forces hard on 5 March. The damage to the pickup truck is extensive, as is the scorching on the rock wall behind it *(Lt Col Scott Campbell)*

Capt Kniep and Maj Clinton arrived over the Shah-i-Kot at sunset. They were followed into Afghan airspace a few hours later by a second pair of A-10s, thus taking the Jacobabad detachment to full strength. Their first exposure to the Shah-i-Kot Valley would see them operating near the 'Whaleback' in response to another TIC, as Capt Kniep recalled;

'After pressing on into Afghanistan, our initial contact was in support of a JTAC [Joint Tactical Air Controller] who had been taking fire. We shared the tasking with a Predator, which was something different for me, as I had never flown with a UAV before. The capabilities it brought to the fight when it came to illuminating the target were outstanding. I could not see the drone, however, and I never did know exactly where it was throughout this particular operation.

'It was tough getting our eyes onto the target, and we had enemy troops pretty close to the friendlies. We were trying to figure out our avenue of attack, as the target area was right in the middle of the mountains. There was a very narrow avenue along which to make an attacking pass – if you got a little off it you could no longer see the target. This was either because of where the UAV was orbiting and how it was illuminating the target, or because of the rugged terrain in the valley. I worked a deconfliction plan in terms of altitude, and we ended up being above the UAV in order to stay away from it while the Predator was attempting to illuminate the target area. Its guidance was critical, as by this time it was pitch black, and Maj Clinton and I had never been in the area before.

'I fired a WP into the area just to confirm that I was seeing what I needed to. Friendlies were two klicks away, and we knew where they were located in relation to the target. Nevertheless, with our narrow avenue of attack, I had to be careful about keeping my eyes on the target and making sure that our bombs were not falling towards the friendlies.

'Again, having never worked with a UAV before, I wanted to be certain that what I was seeing from my vantage point was exactly what the UAV was trying to illuminate, as my field of view on the target was very narrow. Once I fired the rocket the Predator confirmed that I had indeed picked out the target. The problem was that every time I turned I lost sight of it. I finally got to the point where I decided to fly behind my wingman,

chasing him and controlling him as he headed for the target. I was now his FAC(A), and I had him employ his ordnance first. By doing that I could keep my eye both on him and on the illuminated target.

'Whilst still behind Maj Clinton's A-10, I put another WP round down to mark the target. By chasing him, I could tell exactly where his nose was as he dropped two Mk 82 airbursts on the target. I quickly got him deconflicted from me and rolled in and dropped my four Mk 82s, after which he re-attacked with his last two bombs. After that we went to the tanker and then tried to go back into the valley, but the CAOC was worried about how long we had already been airborne and told us to land.'

At Jacobabad, Lt Col Neuenswander was beginning to settle into a routine with the forward deployed elements of the 332nd AEG and the 74th EFS. Seven C-130s had delivered the personnel, bombs and equipment that were needed to operate from the forward location during 5 March, and he now had four A-10s on the ramp, with two more providing cover over the Shah-i-Kot Valley that would also land at Jacobabad following the completion of their tasking. However, the agreement with Pakistan allowed for only five A-10s to be stationed at the base, forcing the two airborne 'Hogs' to divert to Al Udied, in Qatar. Capt Mark Gilchrist was the flight lead for those jets;

'I couldn't believe that they were going to send us back after our mission. Thank God they didn't make us fly all the way back to Al Jaber that night, as I was crushed. We didn't understand why we'd been told to leave. AWACS had relayed to me it was for "diplomatic reasons", but that could have meant anything. I honestly thought for a while I must have seriously screwed something up, and we had been kicked out because of that. We had plenty of time to think about it on the flight back. I thought that the mission had been a complete failure. We didn't find out the real reason until we got back to Al Jaber.'

WORKING WITH THE AC-130

By nightfall on 7 March, Operation *Anaconda* was well into its fifth day, and Capt Campbell was flying for his fourth straight day – the A-10 mission out of Jacobabad that night saw him flying with Capt Ryan Hayden. Weather conditions had deteriorated badly by the time the two 'Hogs' took off, and as the pilots left Pakistan to head to the first tanker in the 'Bigfoot' AAR track, Capts Campbell and Hayden flew into the thick of it. From 14,000 ft up to 24,000 ft, the two heavily loaded A-10s made the slow climb. Carrying six airburst Mk 82s, LAU-131/A rocket pods and a pair of IIR Mavericks to aid their NVGs, the jets made slow progress as they attempted to reach the tanker's altitude.

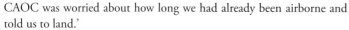

A-10A 79-0223 belonging to the 74th EFS, but wearing markings of sister squadron 75th FS, is prepared for launch from Jacobabad. The crew chief can be seen holding a folded American flag, which many A-10s display on the left side of the cockpit during combat missions. Flying from Pakistan proved to be relatively seamless, and perhaps the biggest problem the detachment faced was when Capt Scott Campbell was intercepted by Pakistani Air Force fighters after returning from a mission. 'They weren't used to the slow speed of the A-10, so they screwed up the intercept and ended up parking in front of me by at least a mile', Capt Campbell recalled. 'I hadn't realised it at the time, but I had just wandered right through the airspace over one of Pakistan's nuclear facilities, which was a big no-no' (Lt Col Mark Gilchrist)

'It was just layer after layer of clouds, and we were all iced over on the climb out of Pakistan', Capt Campbell recalled. 'It was the first time I had actually climbed above the weather and had the ice sublimate. We headed to the tanker track and sure enough there is the "shark fin" – the tanker's vertical stabiliser was sticking out of the top of the clouds! If anybody could find poor weather to rendezvous in it was the tanker guys. We got them to come out of the weather, then refuelled and headed towards the valley'.

Since Capt Campbell's mission on 5 March, al-Qaeda and Taleban forces had altered their tactics, choosing to move in small groups or as individuals, rather than in large concentrations that were easy to spot from the air. They had also learned the significance of WP rockets when they were fired. 'We had to stop putting WPs down to confirm target location, because it didn't take them long to figure out what followed', explained Capt Campbell. 'When the first rocket hit the ground, they scattered in every direction. They knew the guys who were going to get hit were the ones in the largest clump – the higher the number, the larger the target and the higher the probability of a kill. We had to hold back the WP and do our best with talk-ons, thus avoiding the use of rockets. If we saw them we wanted to keep them in a group so that more of them would be killed when we dropped our ordnance. Once they scattered it became more of a problem picking out worthwhile targets to bomb'.

Without a targeting pod, and forced to use the 'poor man's LANTIRN' in the form of the IIR Maverick, A-10 pilots quickly made adjustments to their nocturnal hunting methods. For example, they chose to pair up with AC-130s working in the Shah-i-Kot Valley so as to make use of the gunships' superior sensors. Capt Campbell recalled one such mission on the night of 7 March;

'We worked our way into the valley and under the cloud layer in order to perform FAC(A) for other assets. We had two gunships ("Nail 22" and "Grim 32") operating with us under the layer and a group of F-16s ("Fang 31") who were orbiting above the clouds waiting for targets. We first deconflicted for B-1 "Habu 71", which was going to string JDAMs onto the "Whaleback", making sure the "Vipers" and AC-130s were out of his way. We then made our move to work with the gunships.

'We were able to pick up the two AC-130s in the valley pretty quickly, as they were in their orbits combing the hillsides with their IR floodlights, which we could clearly see through our NVGs. They were putting the "burn" down. It was like two vultures combing the hillsides, the "burn" moving across these hills until it stopped on a target and the 40 mm guns opened fire – *"Wham, Wham"* as the shells hit the ground. The AC-130 was the perfect tool for a permissive environment.

'Working with the gunships was a "win-win" situation for all concerned. The AC-130s had a long vul period to cover, and they were going through a lot of ammunition, especially 40 mm cannon rounds. We had a "bigger bang for the buck" with our 500-lb Mk 82s, our airbursts being more effective than 40 mm rounds if the enemy was spread out. By using our bombs we could make their ammo last longer. Therefore, when we were on station they would use our ammo and we would use their sensors. When we went off station to the tanker, they would hammer away with their cannon once again. So, looking to use our strengths, we joined them on "the perch" – a term we adopted for a tactic that we had devised with the gunship crews during *Anaconda*.

'When employing "the perch", we would stay outside of the AC-130's orbit, flying 1000 ft above the gunship. It proved to be a highly effective tactic that allowed us to hit targets with overwhelming firepower. The gunship would control us and illuminate our targets, either marking the aim point with a couple of 40 mm rounds or using an IR pointer to identify the DMPI [Designated Mean Point of Impact]. We would roll off "the perch", and as soon as we crossed behind the AC-130 and broke their altitude plane, we'd call "Altitude". That was the deconfliction call to let them know that we were breaking their orbit. Immediately, their guns would go cold. I would then roll down the chute, engage the target and then pull off towards the AC-130's tail. As soon as I had crossed behind him I would call "Clear", and the gunship was free to start shooting again.

'On the night of the 7th we started working with "Grim 32", which had located some mortar positions on a hillside. We joined the crew in "the perch" and they put the "burn" onto the targets – thanks to my NVGs I could easily see the DMPI. ETAC "Jaguar 1-2" had plotted and validated the target prior to our arrival overhead. I let "Grim" and "Jaguar" know that I was going to put a couple of Mk 82s on target once we had spun back around the orbit – I wanted to roll in from the west. I called "15 seconds until I'm in", at which point "Stiletto" – a JSTARS operating over the valley – came up on my "freq" and announced that I no longer had permission to drop. I was confused, as not only had "Grim" located and identified the target and the ETAC on the ground validated it, the DMPI was in the middle of a free fire zone for AC-130s! With bombs still onboard, we pushed out for the tanker to refuel and "Grim" was reassigned, leaving the target unserviced.

'When we returned to the valley a short while later, we had "Shocker" flight – a pair of Strike Eagles – above us. We hooked up with "Nail 22" this time and climbed back up to "the perch". Southeast of the "Whaleback", "Nail" found a vehicle under a tarp. They "burned" the target for me and I selected three Mk 82s and rolled in, but I came off dry as I had jammed myself in, never fully rolling out of my banking turn as I followed "Nail" around. I ended up pointing the gun at the truck and squeezed the trigger, but my aim was long by about 40 m. Capt Hayden was cleared in next, and just as he was rolling down the chute he too was called off by "Stiletto" – the JSTARS had received reports that friendly forces had possibly moved into the area.

'We were then pushed to another "freq" to talk to ETAC "White Lightning 20", who reported that his position was 3.5 klicks east of the vehicle we had been targeting.

'Continuing to work with "Nail 22" and the two F-15Es of "Shocker" flight, we were orbiting near the intersections of the passes near Objectives Heather and Ginger when "Shocker" found three vehicles on the move. We passed the information to "Stiletto", seeking their permission to engage, but they told us they had to run the request by "K-Mart" – CAOC's call sign. After 15 minutes there was still no approval and "Shocker" "bingoed" out. Another 15 minutes passed without approval, and by then we too were getting low on gas. Throughout this period we could see "Grim" using its IR sensor to work the nearby ratline south of Ginger. We kept asking "Stiletto" for permission until we had only three minutes of "playtime" left.

"Finally, the JSTARS passed us to "Grim" and "Jaguar 1-2" again. We checked in with the AC-130, and whatever they had gotten into along the ratline had resulted in plenty of secondary explosions. There were dudes trying to run up the sides of this hill as they attempted to flee the gunship's withering fire. We had a much better area weapon with our airburst Mk 82s, so I rolled in and strung six bombs up the hillside in a 300-ft string. Seconds later Capt Hayden rolled in behind me and did the selfsame thing. We repositioned and rolled in again, this time putting about 500 rounds of 30 mm HEI into the hillside. We had dropped 12 Mk 82s and fired almost 1000 rounds of HEI in just a matter of minutes. We asked the gunship crew for BDA and they couldn't see anything. Once the smoke cleared, "Grim" told us that there was nothing moving. Everything was gone. Between the gunship hitting the target with 40 mm cannon rounds and us putting 6000 lbs of ordnance on it, the whole side of the hill was a parking lot.

'From there we pushed out, as I had run us pretty much out of gas. Again, the tanker came forward and got us. We hooked up and went home.'

The weather was no better for Capt Kniep and Lt Col Neuenswander that night when it was their turn to work the valley. Recognising the need for the A-10s, and giving them the appropriate call sign of 'Sandy', JSTARS put Capt Kniep to work organising the airspace over the Shah-i-Kot, as she explained;

'As soon as we arrived on station, "Stiletto" needed to go off station to refuel, so they pretty much handed me the airspace to control. Although I did not have information on where all the aircraft were, that night I controlled 11 different manned types and three UAVs. B-1s and B-52s were coming straight through the valley with TST from the CAOC, and I had to delay their taskings in order to de-conflict their routes with other strike aircraft. I sent Lt Col Neuenswander over onto a back up "freq" as there was too much chatter on the main one, and I made everybody who pushed over to the Strike "freq" go to his frequency, where he was "racking and stacking" them for me. I would then let him know who I wanted, when I wanted them and where I wanted them. He would then push them over to the Strike "freq" and they would come in and talk to me. I would control them in onto the target, working with an ETAC on the ground.

'At one point we had received partial information relating to what appeared to be enemy forces on the move, and we started pulling together all the pieces of intelligence we had. Typically, I had nine of the ten "pieces of the puzzle" that I needed to confirm that they were indeed enemy fighters. The one piece that was missing was a friendly patrol that had not checked in, and we did not know where they were located. This fact did not sit well with me. The patrol could have easily been in the vicinity of enemy forces, as its last known position was just a couple of klicks away from the targets we were looking at.

'As the situation developed, I was under a lot of pressure to authorise an attack on what appeared to be an enemy position. I held everybody

31

off, however, while I tried to confirm that last piece of information, and it turned out that the "enemy position" was in fact the missing friendly patrol. Everything was so fluid during *Anaconda*, and TF Mountain HQ could not keep track of everything that was going on. On this occasion situational awareness (SA) had been lost in respect to the location of the missing patrol.

'We have a checklist we go through that we have been trained to follow when it comes to target recognition, and you are taught that you don't skip steps of the checklist. In that kind of environment where people are screaming at you to clear them "Hot" to attack, it is really easy to skip steps in order to get ordnance on the ground that much quicker. That is when we make mistakes. Even when talking to the ETACs on the ground that night, they too were convinced that they were looking at an enemy position.'

The five A-10s continued to fly from Jacobabad until 9 March, when the jets and personnel began to return to Al Jaber. The pressure of having American combat aircraft flying from its soil had finally become too much for the Pakistani government, and with the US Army at last having a firm grasp on *Anaconda*, the decision was made to send the A-10s back to Kuwait. Upon departing Pakistan, the 'Hogs' would fly one last mission over the Shah-i-Kot Valley before returning to Al Jaber. However, getting out of Pakistan would prove almost as difficult as getting into the country, as Lt Col Neuenswander recalled;

'The people there that we had borrowed the radios from were asking for their stuff back as we were packing up to leave. I told them they could have the radios two hours after the last A-10 had departed. So, two hours and ten minutes later, a single A-10 showed up back in the pattern. Even before the jet had landed I got a phone call from the air attaché at the US ambassador's office in Pakistan. He told me that the ambassador and the President of the United States wanted that A-10 out of there. My response was that I didn't even know why it had come back here. I told them that I would have to call them back. Then the CAOC called, telling me that I had to get that aeroplane out of there. At that point I still didn't know what was wrong as we didn't have any radios anymore!

'Well, the problem was that the jet's refuelling door was not working, and the A-10 could not make it back to Al Jaber without a top off from the tanker. Our maintenance people were telling us it was parts plus twelve hours to fix it. We went back up to the mission planning computers and figured out that if we took all the ordnance off the jet, it could fly to Seeb, in Oman, and refuel on the ground there. And that is what we did.'

Four of the five A-10s to make the trip from Kuwait to Jacobabad can be seen in this image. A-10 support was critical, with five jets providing 21 hours of continuous CAS and FAC(A) duties over the Shah-i-Kot during initial support of *Anaconda*. The five 'Hogs' would leave Pakistan on 9 March after a week of flying combat missions from Jacobabad *(Lt Col Mark Gilchrist)*

BAGRAM

The first A-10 pilot to fly into Bagram, in Afghanistan, was Lt Col John Horner. Arriving aboard a C-17, he immediately went about his assigned taskings – helping to get the air campaign back on track during *Anaconda* and preparing the battered ex-Afghan air force base for the A-10s that were to arrive here within a few weeks. The latter assignment would be the more difficult of the two.

Situated 25 miles north of Afghanistan's capital of Kabul, the airfield sat at an altitude of 5000 ft surrounded by the Hindu Kush mountains. It had been the hub of Soviet activity following the country's invasion of Afghanistan in 1979. However, by March 2002 the condition of Bagram was anything but optimal. The poor craftsmanship of Soviet-era structures, years of neglect and a decade of civil war had reduced the airfield to an almost useless state. Bombed-out buildings, thousands upon thousands of mines, unexploded ordnance (UXO), destroyed aircraft and abandoned vehicles littered the airfield. To make matters worse, there was no perimeter security, which meant people were allowed to wander around the base unchallenged.

'I had been working at the CAOC at Prince Sultan Air Base, where I was in a strategy cell helping to create a classified project that would become Operation *Iraqi Freedom* (OIF)', recalled Lt Col Horner. 'One of the pillars of the strategy I favoured from an A-10 perspective was as the ground forces moved through an area, we would forward base jets at captured airfields. Whilst I was pushing this idea Gen Moseley got wind of it, and knowing that *Anaconda* could not be supported entirely from Kuwait, he threw me and another colonel forward to help with the battle, and see if Bagram could house A-10s.

On 23 March 2002 Lt Col Arden Dahl landed the first A-10A at Bagram, leading his 74th EFS on its second OEF detachment since arriving at Al Jaber in late February for what had originally been planned as a routine OSW deployment. As Lt Col Dahl taxied to the ramp a rainbow appeared in the background. The arriving A-10 pilots and groundcrews considered this to be a very good omen for the mission that lay ahead of them *(Matt Neuenswander)*

'The real heroes of those early days in March 2002 were from the Missouri ANG airfield operations unit, and they were instrumental in helping get the A-10s into Bagram.'

On 18 March Lt Col Neuenswander and Capts Kniep and Campbell arrived at Bagram as part of the 74th EFS's advanced contingent (ADVON), helping Lt Col Horner in the final stages of base preparation prior to the first A-10s arriving four days later. Lt Col Arden Dahl, commanding officer of the 74th EFS, landed the first of six 'Hogs' to arrive at Bagram on 22 March. Watching this historic event take place, Lt Col Horner was a little concerned about the state of the runway, as he explained;

'The huge issue with the runway was that it was not well built. I had no engineering analysis of its condition other than me walking out there and, using my experiences as a high-time A-10 guy, saying "this will work"! It had potholes that were four to six inches deep in places, and driving over it was like riding down a bumpy country road. My biggest fear was the first aeroplane would come in and strip its gear off, with the same fate befalling the other five jets as they landed behind it. What would become of my life if that happened?!'

For a group of pilots that had deployed to well-prepared bases in Europe, Saudi Arabia and Kuwait, the challenges and obstacles of Bagram were unique. No running water at first, the mandatory burning of human waste and living in tents that were either too cold or too hot. 'Bagram was an interesting place', recalled Capt Anthony Roe, weapons officer with the 74th EFS. 'There were UXOs everywhere, and you never walked on anything that was not a hardened surface or an area that had been cleared.

This view of the living area for the first USAF personnel to arrive at Bagram for the A-10 deployment was taken from the control tower. As can be clearly seen, conditions at the air base were basic in the extreme. The temporary A-10 operations centre was housed in the light salmon-coloured building to the left of the photograph. Tents with basic heating elements provided shelter for personnel, food took the form of MREs (Meals, Ready-to-Eat) and showers consisted of baby wipes in the early days. 'It was a bit of a shock', explained Lt Col Horner. 'We had become a force that had grown used to American bases stateside and in Europe, and when we deployed to the Middle East we used modern facilities in Saudi Arabia, Kuwait or Qatar. Bagram was definitely not any of those *(Matt Neuenswander)*

Lt Cols Matt Neuenswander (left), Bob Silva (centre) and John Horner (right) pose with members of the Northern Alliance who guarded the A-10 bomb dump. These Afghans actually lived within the bomb dump, and received $100 a month for their services *(Matt Neuenswander)*

Burned out and blown up tanks and half-tracks still littered the sides of the main road and Northern Alliance soldiers could still be found wandering freely on base toting their AK-47s. We referred to Bagram as the "bar scene from *Star Wars*".

When the A-10s arrived the US Army believed it had been given their own personal 'air force', and Lt Col Neuenswander had to fight daily battles to keep – at least from the USAF's perspective – Bagram from becoming the 'Wild, Wild West'. Recognising the need to have a 'full bird' colonel leading the new air group that was to be activated, the air force duly promoted Neuenswander to the rank of colonel. His job was to ensure the smooth running of the unit, despite the challenges presented by its coexistence at Bagram. Capt Campbell detailed some of the issues facing the new group;

'"Big Green" (US Army) had just got to Bagram, and before that it was "Big SOF". The base was still a bit uncontrolled. When we first set up, SOF guys would routinely run out onto the runway, getting in your way. It was not like I had a horn on the aeroplane! We ended up bringing in our own air force cops, and we put concertina wire around our ramp and created an entry control point [ECP]. The Army lost their mind over that! You would have thought we had dropped an F-bomb in church. They just couldn't believe we were going to restrict their movements, but air force cops see it their way, and their way only.'

Clearing the runway from foreign object debris (FOD), both day and night, was a monumental task. Everything from 55 gallon drums to grenades unearthed by mine clearing operations found their way onto the runway. Capt Kniep remembers one FOD trip with Capt Campbell;

'We were in a golf cart, and we started picking up tiny pebbles, and before we had gone five feet down the runway our entire cart was full. It got to the point where we would pick up a rock and decide if we could actually drive safely over it or not. We learned really quickly that we could indeed live with a lot of smaller debris on the runway.'

The A-10s were now much closer to the fight, and aircraft were maintained on alert at Bagram ready to support the troops on the ground. The 'Hog' had taken up residence in Afghanistan.

SAVING LIVES

The arrival of the A-10 at Bagram was keenly anticipated by both the ADVON team of the 74th EFS, who was preparing the facility for its aircraft, and the US Army personnel who were beginning to flow back in from the Shah-i-Kot Valley following the official conclusion of Operation *Anaconda*. For those who had witnessed the prowess of the Pakistan-based A-10s during CAS missions flown during March 2002, this move to permanently locate the aircraft within Afghanistan itself was a welcome measure. Indeed, for one soldier from TF Mountain returning to Bagram, his survival of *Anaconda* was due directly to the 'Hog's' timely intervention in the the Shah-i-Kot, as Col Neuenswander recalled*(text continues on page 44)*;

COLOUR PLATES

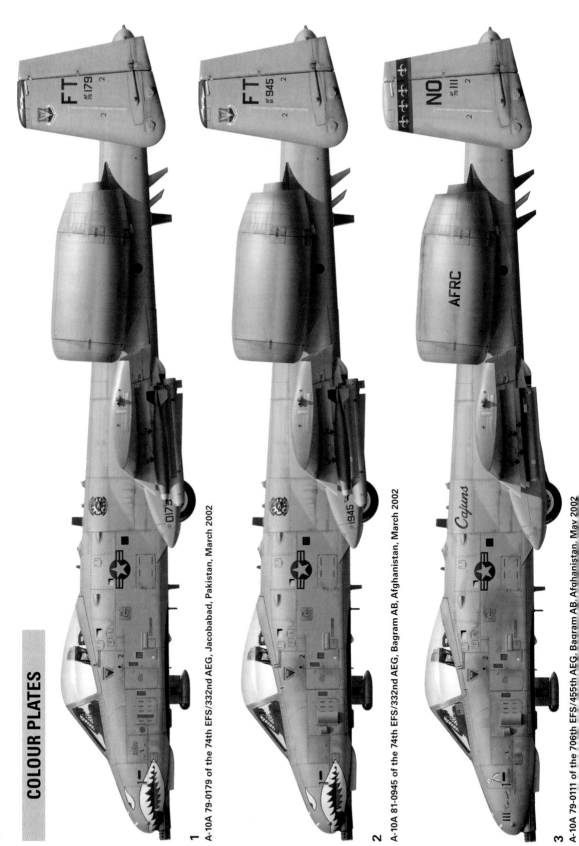

1
A-10A 79-0179 of the 74th EFS/332nd AEG, Jacobabad, Pakistan, March 2002

2
A-10A 81-0945 of the 74th EFS/332nd AEG, Bagram AB, Afghanistan, March 2002

3
A-10A 79-0111 of the 706th EFS/455th AEG, Bagram AB, Afghanistan, May 2002

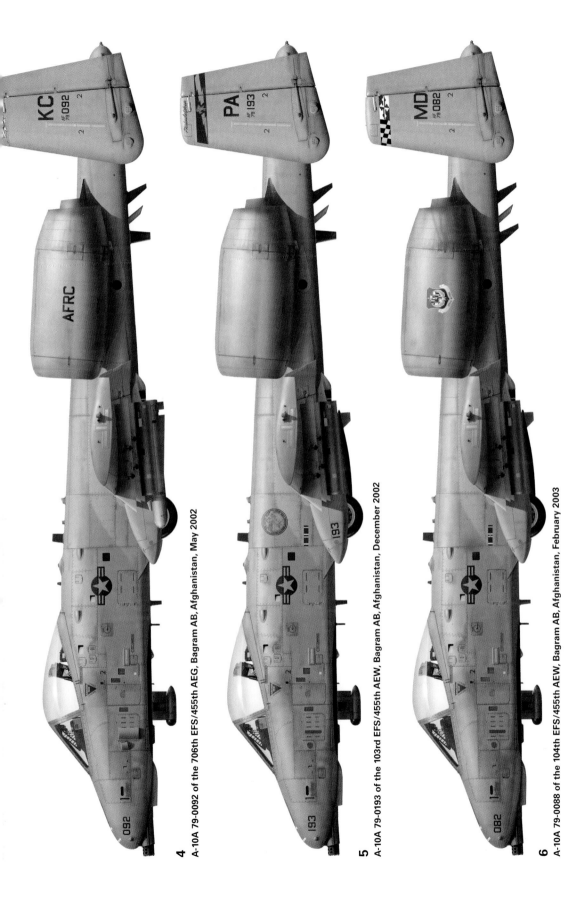

4

A-10A 79-0092 of the 706th EFS/455th AEG, Bagram AB, Afghanistan, May 2002

5

A-10A 79-0193 of the 103rd EFS/455th AEW, Bagram AB, Afghanistan, December 2002

6

A-10A 79-0088 of the 104th EFS/455th AEW, Bagram AB, Afghanistan, February 2003

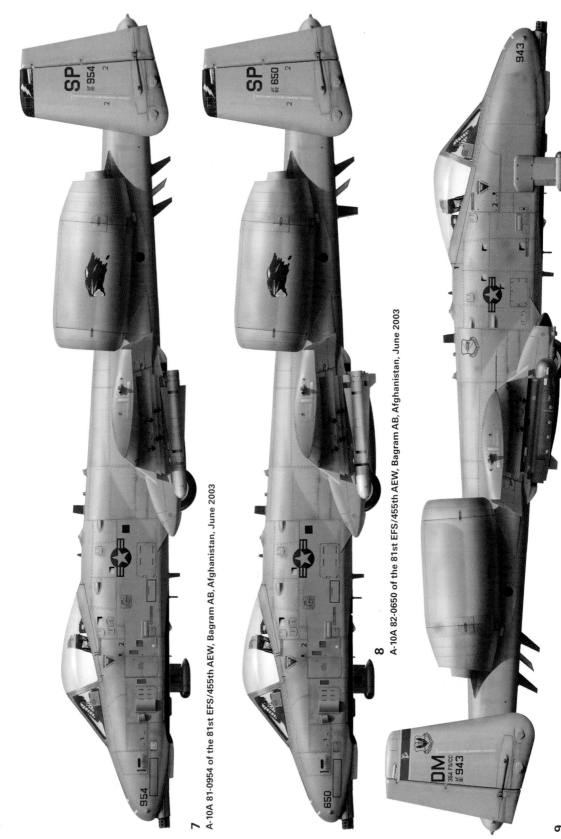

7
A-10A 81-0954 of the 81st EFS/455th AEW, Bagram AB, Afghanistan, June 2003

8
A-10A 82-0650 of the 81st EFS/455th AEW, Bagram AB, Afghanistan, June 2003

9
A-10A 81-0943 of the 354th EFS/455th AEW, Bagram AB, Afghanistan, November 2003

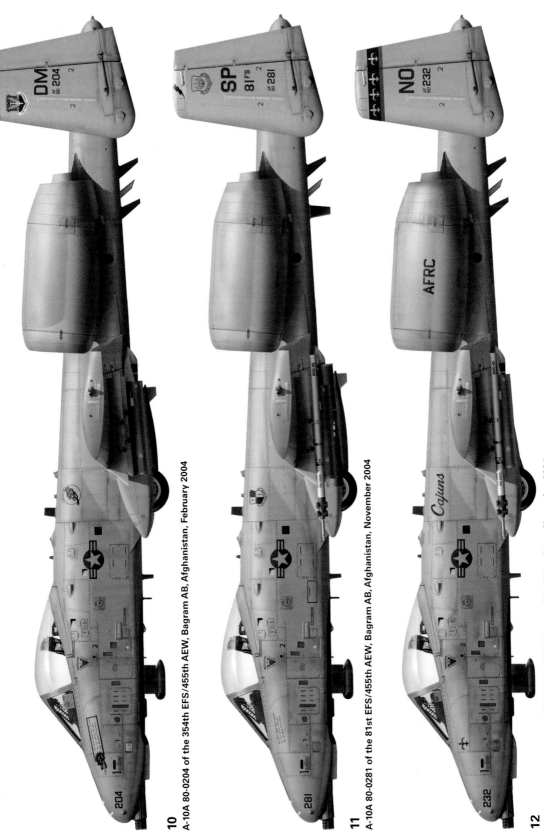

10
A-10A 80-0204 of the 354th EFS/455th AEW, Bagram AB, Afghanistan, February 2004

11
A-10A 80-0281 of the 81st EFS/455th AEW, Bagram AB, Afghanistan, November 2004

12
A-10A 80-0232 of the 81st EFS/455th AEW, Bagram AB, Afghanistan, November 2004

39

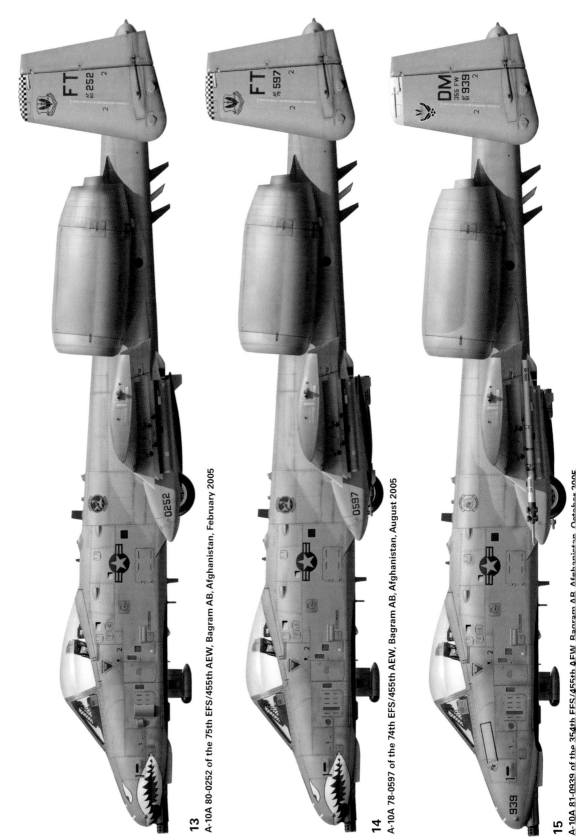

13
A-10A 80-0252 of the 75th EFS/455th AEW, Bagram AB, Afghanistan, February 2005

14
A-10A 78-0597 of the 74th EFS/455th AEW, Bagram AB, Afghanistan, August 2005

15
A-10A 81-0939 of the 354th EFS/455th AEW, Bagram AB, Afghanistan, October 2005

16
A-10A 79-0187 of the 355th EFS/455th AEW, Bagram AB, Afghanistan, February 2006

17
A-10A 81-0995 of the 355th EFS/455th AEW, Bagram AB, Afghanistan, April 2006

18
A-10A 81-0963 of the 81st EFS/455th AEW, Bagram AB, Afghanistan, June 2006

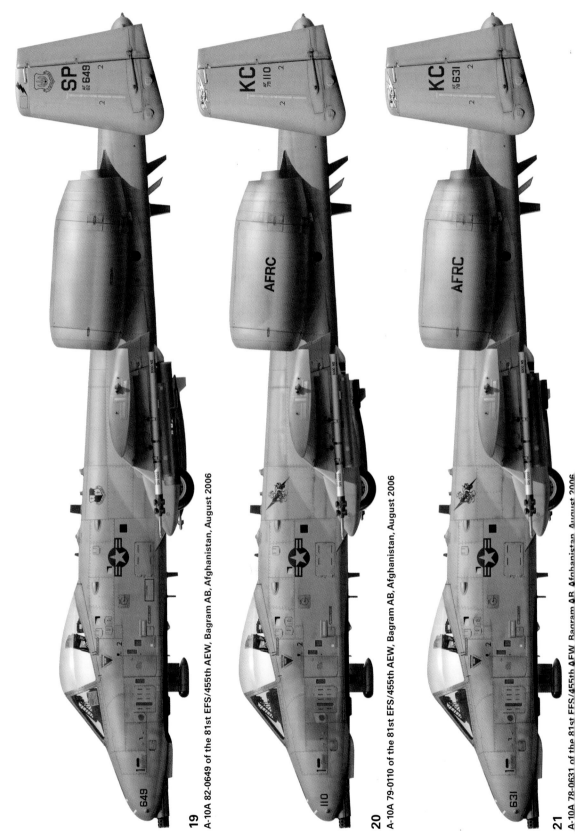

19
A-10A 82-0649 of the 81st EFS/455th AEW, Bagram AB, Afghanistan, August 2006

20
A-10A 79-0110 of the 81st EFS/455th AEW, Bagram AB, Afghanistan, August 2006

21
A-10A 78-0631 of the 81st EFS/455th AEW, Bagram AB, Afghanistan, August 2006

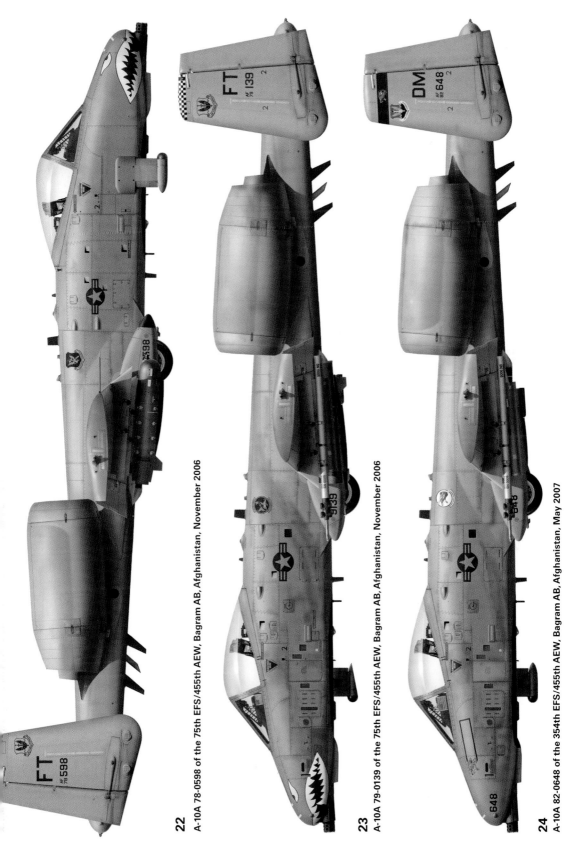

22
A-10A 78-0598 of the 75th EFS/455th AEW, Bagram AB, Afghanistan, November 2006

23
A-10A 79-0139 of the 75th EFS/455th AEW, Bagram AB, Afghanistan, November 2006

24
A-10A 82-0648 of the 354th EFS/455th AEW, Bagram AB, Afghanistan, May 2007

'I was with a few airmen digging a latrine – one of the thousands of things that needed to be completed before the A-10s arrived – when I was approached by a soldier. I was in a pair of Battle Dress Uniform pants, a t-shirt, no hat and with no rank tabs on. This young specialist from the 10th Mountain showed up and said he was looking for the A-10 commander. I replied, "Well you found him son. How can I help you?" Frankly, I felt really bad at this point because I had just been forced to put barbed wire up around my camp – not to keep my people in, but to stop the young army guys from stealing us blind. So my feelings towards this young soldier weren't too positive, as I was sure he was here to steal something.

'He replied, "My dad says that I need to find the A-10 guys and tell them my story". I asked him what was going on and he told me, "We were out there during *Anaconda* and you guys saved my life". He proceeded to explain to us that he and his platoon were trapped in the floor of the Shah-i-Kot Valley, and the bad guys were walking mortars in towards them. They were pretty sure that the enemy had them ranged, and that they were all going to die. Then two A-10s came over and

Sitting at a very empty Bagram AB on 24 March 2002 is A-10A 80-0172. Part of the first detachment of 'Hogs' sent to Afghanistan from Al Jaber AB the previous day, the jet had commenced flying missions less than 24 hours after arriving at Bagram. Although activity in-country post-*Anaconda* was considerably reduced, the A-10 is still carrying weapons on ten of an available eleven hardpoints. Note the AN/AAS-35(V) Pave Penny laser spot tracker on its dedicated pylon beneath the cockpit *(Matt Neuenswander)*

On 30 March 2002 Hamid Karzai and his advisors visited Bagram AB and the 74th EFS, the unit giving them a close look at A-10A 79-0186. At the time Karzai was Chairman of the Interim Administration, which evolved into the current Afghan government *(Matt Neuenswander)*

melted the mortar team. The jets dropped their ordnance and then went back about their business. When the soldier got pulled out of the valley, he had had the chance to talk to his dad, and he told him he thought the A-10s were coming in to Bagram.

'Well, it turned out that his dad was Robert "Muck" Brown, a real icon in the A-10 community. Well respected and loved by everybody associated with the "Hog", he and I were close friends who had served together at England AFB, in Louisiana, many years before OEF. At home, I had a photograph of me holding this little boy and my son in front of an A-10 at England AFB when he was four or five years old. I did not recognise him now, as stood in front of me was a 23-year-old grown man.

'When you are up there and you hear grown men yelling for help on the radio, you never fully realise just how intense the situation on the ground is until one of those involved comes and tells you, "You saved my life". Our whole air force career, we are trained to mitigate risk when in combat, always have an alternate plan and not to over-fly your gas. During *Anaconda* we broke every rule we had because guys were dying in the valley. We had no alternate. You just never knew who it was you were saving.'

455th AEW

On 26 April 2002 the detachment of A-10s belonging to the 332nd AEG from Al Jaber was re-designated the 455th Air Expeditionary Wing (AEW), and Col Neuenswander became its first commanding officer. He was subsequently replaced by Col Marcel Kerdavid, a Massachusetts ANG A-10 pilot who would become CO of the wing on 26 July 2002. The army would have its A-10s and the air force could begin to shape the air war from Bagram.

With the departure of the 74th EFS in late March, the first 'Rainbow' team (a detachment consisting of jets and crews from more than one unit) arrived at Bagram, consisting of six jets. These aircraft were supplied from two AFRes units, namely the 303rd FS at Whiteman AFB, Missouri, and the 706th FS at NAS JRB New Orleans, and when combined they formed the 706th EFS. The 303rd supplied two A-10s and the 706th four, and the squadron operated from Bagram for nearly 90 days. There was very little ordnance dropped during their time at Bagram, however. The aircraft were initially flown in CAP-style missions, where they would head to an assigned area and hold, on call in case a situation developed where they were needed – either to provide show of force or for kinetic employment. At this point in 2002, the number of US troops in-theatre was quite small, and overwatch for their limited areas of operation was easily achievable.

For the pilots of the 706th EFS, the biggest danger they faced was operating from the runway at

Capt Rich Erkkila, a pilot with the 354th EFS, pre-flights an AGM-65D Maverick missile hanging from his A-10A. The IR Maverick was the 'poor man's targeting pod' prior to the 'Hog' community being issued with the vastly superior Litening pod. Pilots complained that using the Maverick's IR sensor was like looking through a soda straw at the target. Yet despite the AGM-65D's unsuitability for nighttime precision targeting operations, it was better than nothing *(USAF)*

Bagram, especially after they were tasked with initiating night operations from the base. 303rd FS pilot Maj Brian Borgen participated in this deployment;

'The biggest thing the reserve component did was that we moved into the night realm – it was all day flying when we arrived. When we were asked to perform night sorties, our biggest concern was the condition of the runway. It was still in bad shape, being in a state of near disrepair. Being an AFRes unit, we had a pretty good experience base to call on for night operations, and I think that was why we were given approval by the CAOC to fly these missions. I really feel that if the runway had indeed been inspected by senior officers from off-base, I don't think they would have allowed us to fly.

'Our greatest achievement during our three months at Bagram was getting 24-hour A-10 coverage started over Afghanistan. The unit took a progressive approach to completing this task, as we had to sell it to our superiors due to the significant risks associated with operating from the base's substandard runway at night. We spent a lot of time working out how we were going to safely use the runway, which literally had holes in it on both sides at different points. We started slowly and then increased the mission tempo until we reached a normal operating pace.

'We had to takeoff and land using NVGs as the runway was not lit. The driver of the pickup trick that took us to and from the jets also used an NVG monocle, which he would hold up to his eye whilst on the move! On no-moon nights we really could not see anything until we were literally right on top of the jets.'

On 23 August the pioneering 706th EFS was replaced by the 354th FS from Davis-Monthan AFB, the latter unit making the largest contingency deployment of A-10s since Operation *Desert Shield/Storm* in 1990-91. Twenty 'Hogs' would make the trip, and the force would be split between Al Jaber, where the aircraft would help enforce the no-fly zone over southern Iraq as part of OSW, and Bagram. Lt Col Tim Stafford was the squadron commander and Lt Col Wade Thompson his deputy. The latter spent his first six weeks in Al Jaber, before switching locations with his commanding officer on 15 October.

Afghanistan remained very quiet following *Anaconda*. Lt Col Thompson would fly 38 night missions prior to leaving Bagram on 11 December, and during this time he employed ordnance twice as much as any other pilot in the squadron – he dropped bombs on just two occasions;

'The second time I engaged the enemy was on 23 November near Lwara, right up alongside the Pakistani border. A FOB near there had been taking rocket fire, and a ground patrol had the site of the launcher in view. An ETAC began talking me on, and he started giving me a 9-line brief. The enemy was 75 m away from his group of friendlies, and he was asking for me to drop a bomb, which I was not going to do due to his close proximity to the enemy. He then asked for the gun, and I began to set up for a pass. However, I was nervous about strafing that close at night when I was unsure of the target elevation. I asked the ETAC if the patrol could move back, and he said that they could. Apparently, they had all-terrain vehicles, because in the space of just two minutes they were a klick away, and were marking their new position with an IR strobe.

While self-protection flares were designed to protect low-flying A-10s from heat-seeking surface-to-air missiles, they have often been used to protect ground forces in OEF. 'Hog' pilots would make low passes over closely engaged forces and deploy flares, causing the enemy to cease firing and take cover. This often provided Coalition forces with a moment to disengage, or convinced the Taleban to break off their attack altogether *(Gary Wetzel)*

'I dropped a LUU-19 flare so that I could set myself up with better SA. Flying this close to the border, I wanted to make sure that I did not expend any ordnance inside Pakistan. Happy with the target marking, and its position in relation to the border, I swung around and dropped one Mk 82 airburst bomb. The rocket fire immediately stopped.

'My most memorable, and satisfying, mission came nine days later, and saw me expend no ordnance. On 2 December, whilst flying another night sortie, I got a call on Guard [emergency radio frequency] from "Playboy 1-4", who was asking for a "Sandy". He was a JTAC who had been operating with SOF team "White Horse 2-3" up near Jalalabad, and we were south of Kabul near Gardez. They had been ambushed, resulting in the JTAC losing contact with his SOF team. He could talk to us, but not to "White Horse 2-3".

'The weather in the area was bad that night, with the ceiling at around 10,000 ft. I could see a hole in the clouds, which I "split-essed" through in order to get beneath it. I took his coordinates and plugged them in and we were able to fly directly over his position. He asked us to pop some flares so that he could see us. Once he saw them the JTAC requested that we kept on popping flares as he hoped that this would scare off the Taleban who had occupied a nearby ridgeline. We spent between 45 minutes to an hour performing a series of passes, dropping flares as we went. We finally got the JTAC reunited with his SOF team, the latter having been on the other side of the ridgeline, about a mile away – I have no idea how they got separated by such a distance. By this time we had burned way down on our gas, and I ended up landing back at Bagram on emergency fuel.'

The 103rd, 104th and 81st EFSs that subsequently served at Bagram for varying periods of time from December 2002 through to November 2003 saw only limited action, as the Taleban remained

The AN/AAQ-28 Litening II targeting pod revolutionised the way the A-10A was employed in Afghanistan. Having served ANG and AFRes units well in OIF in 2003, the pod was issued to active-duty A-10 squadrons later that same year. Indeed, the 354th FS gave the system its combat debut with the A-10 in OEF from October 2003, although the unit only had sufficient pods to equip aircraft flown by flight leads *(USAF)*

largely inactive. Nevertheless, the units in-theatre steadily improved the base infrastructure and honed their operational skills with ground units patrolling throughout Afghanistan.

LITENING STRIKES

The key operational theatre for A-10 units in 2003-04 was Iraq following the launching of OIF in March 2003. From October of that year, several ANG and AFRes 'Hog' squadrons flew combat missions with aircraft that were equipped with an AN/AAQ-28 Litening II targeting pod (TGP). The latter greatly improved the A-10's war-fighting capability, even if only a fraction of the pod's targeting capacity could be utilised by 'Hog' pilots due to their jets' ancient avionics making cockpit methodology difficult.

The TGP was the right solution for most of the missions the A-10 would be flying in both OIF and OEF, the pod providing the pilot with a forward-looking infrared (FLIR) sensor, laser designator, laser range finder and stabilised target tracking. The quality of these systems was appreciably better than the IIR Maverick missile sensor that pilots had been using at night up until then. There were limitations to the Litening's incorporation, however, beginning with the way the pod was attached to the A-10. Although Maverick missiles were usually carried on either station's three or nine, the TGP had to be hung on one of these hardpoints – primarily station nine – so that the A-10 was tricked into thinking the pod was an IIR AGM-65D missile. As a result, pilots found switchology difficult to master, especially when self-lasing a target due to the lack of TGP information on the Head-up Display (HUD).

In October 2003, the 354th FS deployed from Davis-Monthan AFB for split operations at Bagram and Kirkuk, in Iraq. Once in-theatre, they became the first active duty A-10s to employ targeting pods in combat. At first there were not enough TGPs for every jet to fly with one fitted, so typically the flight lead's aircraft carried a pod and the wingman's did not. 'At night the pod worked pretty well', explained Lt Col John Horner, CO of the 354th during this deployment. 'With the IR marker you could point out things to your wingman, who was on NVGs and could therefore see the beam from the TGP. During daylight, however, the challenge was sharing this same information with your wingman, as he could not see the IR marker with the naked eye. The pod allowed us to be more effective in the way we executed some of the specific mission sets in OEF, such as convoy escort, recce runs and overwatch.'

Lt Col Horner was a great fan of the A-10's 'forward-firing arsenal', namely its rockets, Maverick missiles and gun. And during a mission in late 2003 he became one of the few 'Hog' pilots to have employed an AGM-65 in Afghanistan

'We were working a JAAT [Joint Air Attack Tactics] with some Apaches, trying to target some folks that had pinned down an American patrol with gunfire from within a mud compound. We were cycling in and shooting the gun, but not getting the weapons effect we wanted. The ETAC we were working with was one of the senior controllers from the ASOC, and he knew that we had Mavericks in our quiver and requested one. We had to coordinate the shot, as the ground team needed to pull some guys back a few hundred metres from the compound wall before we fired the weapon.

'I pressed in, but we had bad comms and I did not get clearance to fire, so I came off dry from that first pass. I made a teardrop turn and then came back on the attack axis, placing the Maverick cue over the spot in the compound that I wanted to hit with the missile. This time I got clearance "hot", and let the weapon rip. The Maverick hit the compound precisely where it was needed. We followed up with a few more strafing runs before heading home.'

PAVE PENNY

The first Pave Penny laser spot tracker (LST) was delivered to the USAF in March 1977, the AN/AAS-35(V), as it was designated, being attached to a small pylon on the right side of the A-10 directly below the cockpit. PAVE later became the designation for Precision Avionics Vectoring Equipment, and the pod was designed to work day or night detecting the reflection of a laser beam containing the correct four-digit target code. The pod would then produce a symbol in the HUD to pinpoint the target's location.

Although an ageing system by the time the A-10 was introduced to combat in OEF, Pave Penny still proved its worth on numerous occasions over Afghanistan. One pilot to make use of the LST was Capt Andrew Stone of the 354th FS at Davis-Monthan AFB. In March 2004 he had received a temporary assignment to the Alaska-based 355th FS, which had been tasked with performing back-to-back Air Expeditionary Force (AEF) cycles at Bagram from 26 March through to 1 October 2004. Capt Stone was a Weapons Officer, and he was replacing squadronmate Capt Jonathan Scheer who, whilst temporarily assigned to the 355th, had been killed on the night of 25 February 2004 when his A-10 crashed shortly after takeoff from the unit's home at Eielson AFB.

Although the Pave Penny may not have been optimal for every mission in OEF, there were times when the pod was the best tool for the job, as Capt Stone found out once in-theatre;

'We were re-tasked after takeoff to take out this radio repeater site on top of a jagged, craggy mountain. It was being used to broadcast voice transmissions from one enemy commander to another. We had just launched on a dawn patrol mission when we received the tasking, and we reached the target area just before daybreak. A Predator was already on station, the UAV using its IR marker to show us approximately where the repeater was. I did everything I could with my Litening pod's laser designator in an effort to locate the target, talking to the Predator controller, who was thousands of miles away. I was still struggling to locate it when the sun came up, at which point we lost the ability to use his IR marker to spot where the target was supposed to be.

'We were awaiting approval to hit the repeater during the target talk. Indeed, I was seeking this approval whilst simultaneously trying to locate the repeater! I decided to hand over the laser designating of the target to the Predator, while I dialed up the Pave Penny and had it look at a certain area in the HUD. The Litening pod was great at acquiring laser energy, but in the A-10A it did not present it accurately in the HUD. This meant that you could not use it for laser spot tracking.

'I knew that the Pave Penny was looking in the general area that the Predator was lasing, so I told its operator that I was ten seconds out, tracker on. Coming in from the south, I got a spot. Sometimes the Pave Penny would settle down pretty quickly on the target, but on other occasions it was erratic and would not lock on well at all. The Pave Penny's biggest problem was that it didn't see the laser energy until you were rolled in and established down the "chute", heading for the target. It could take two to three seconds for the Pave Penny to acquire the laser energy and then present its laser spot tracking diamond in the HUD over the target. You then had to manoeuvre the jet to get either the gun cross or weapons pipper on the target and then effectively deliver your ordnance.

'Sometimes, your pass at the target had to aborted because of the inability of the Pave Penny to acquire the laser energy fast enough. On other occasions the attack run fell down simply through miscommunication. This happened when I went after the repeater. I rolled in, only to suffer a bad radio link with the Predator controller. It took us a couple of passes to get our timing worked out so that he could provide us with the laser energy we required to hit the target. I never did see the radio repeater, as it was literally only a whip antenna – from the heights we were operating at we were never going to be able to see it. We were talking about something the size of a broom stick! We strafed the target area several times using the Pave Penny to guide us in, but were not able to take the repeater out – in my opinion, a radio repeater is the hardest target to hit!'

'BLACKWATER 61'

At 0740 hrs on 27 November 2004 a CASA C-212-200 twin turboprop transport aircraft departed Bagram on a re-supply mission to an austere US Army forward operating base (FOB) at Farah, 450 miles to the southwest. In addition to carrying 400 lbs of illumination mortars for the site, the aircraft had three crewmen and three US Army soldiers on board, the latter hitching a ride back to their units at Farah. About 45 minutes later, the C-212 crashed into Baba Mountain at a height of nearly 14,700 ft – almost 2000 ft below its summit. The aircraft was being flown by two experienced pilots who, conversely, had only recently arrived in Afghanistan – they had each completed about 30 hours in-country. The C-212 would not be reported missing for nearly eight hours, at which point a search and rescue (SAR) operation was initiated.

Lt Col Ronald Miller was the commanding officer of the 706th FS, the AFRes reserve squadron based at NAS JRB New Orleans. Lt Col Miller had arrived in-theatre with six A-10s to augment the deployment of the 81st FS from Spangdahlem, Germany, in September 2004, these units relieving the 355th FS. This deployment would be the 706th's second, and last, to Bagram, as it would fall victim to the 2005 Base Realignment and Closure Commission and Hurricane 'Katrina'.

Lt Col Miller's flight on 28 November was to be his last from Bagram, and before he took off at around 0200 hrs that morning, he and his wingman were re-rolled into the SAR mission to find 'Blackwater 61'. The main search effort was concentrated along the expected flightpath of the C-212, and Lt Col Miller was also supplied with an Iridium satellite phone with which he was to try and call the crew of the downed aircraft.

The A-10 pilots began their search for the aircraft using the age old technique of searching grid patterns, as Lt Col Miller recalled;

'Using the search patterns, we picked up a beacon transmitting on civilian Guard 121.5. Unable to steer directly towards the beacon, we flew until the transmission grew louder. Then, when it began to get softer, we marked the spot, changed direction and flew towards the signal again until it became stronger once more. When it again got softer we marked another spot. Having repeated this routine several times, we eventually worked our way down to within a few hundred metres of the crash site. Running that beacon down took about 30 minutes from when we first heard it.

'Using the targeting pod, we scoured the mountainside for signs of wreckage. There was no thermal imagery out there at all, as the beacon was located near the top of a mountain that was being lashed by 40 mph winds which were blowing so much snow around that we could not ID anything. I climbed up to a higher altitude so that I could have line-of-sight with the ASOC, and I told my controller that he needed to redirect the rescue effort. It took a lot of convincing on my part to have it moved over to that part of the country.

'Nobody thought the C-212 was there, and initially ASOC believed that we were getting spurious signals on our radios. That was when I reminded them that there was only one civilian aircraft flying in-country that day, and I was listening to a beacon transmitting on civilian Guard. I suggested politely that they might want to come over and listen to this, which they eventually did. After sunrise, ASOC brought in a MC-130, which did indeed find the wreckage. It took two more days to reach the site, as the aircraft had crashed in a very remote location blighted by poor weather. Unfortunately, no one aboard the aeroplane survived.'

FOLLOWING THE ROE

Afghanistan's border with Pakistan stretches for more than 1500 miles, and it is notoriously porous. Following the launch of OEF and the initial pressure applied by the Northern Alliance and US forces, surviving members of the Taleban and al-Qaeda fled across the Afghan border into the Federally Administered Tribal Areas (FATA) of northwestern Pakistan. Officially, this region is a semi-autonomous area, but such an assessment is overly optimistic. Of the seven agencies, or tribal districts, in the FATA, the agencies of North and South Waziristan are the most notorious for their collection

Senior Airman Sterling Scales loads a WP (phosphorous) rocket into a LAU-131/A launcher attached to the wing pylon of an A-10 from the 354th EFS *(USAF)*

of enemy combatants. They also contain hundreds of trails that lead into Afghanistan, allowing for the re-supply of personnel and equipment.

Trying to stem this flow of men and materiel both by day and by night is not an easy job, although it is a mission that all A-10 units in-theatre have been tasked with performing since 2002. One pilot to fly myriad border patrols was Maj Barry Coggins of the 74th EFS, his unit having replaced the 75th EFS at Bagram in May 2005 following the latter unit's five-month tour in-theatre;

'You hear the expression cigarettes can kill you, and that is a true statement, especially at night along the Afghan-Pakistan border. Under NVGs you could see little light blooms near the border, and when you put your targeting pod on a bloom, you could see on the cockpit display someone sitting on the ground smoking a cigarette. Admittedly, the imagery did not exactly look like someone sitting there enjoying a cigarette, but if you watched the screen long enough you would see the cigarette bloom blossom up in size and then fade out. A minute later this would be repeated as the smoker took another drag.

'It wasn't hard to find people waiting to cross the border. You would mark the blooms' location, and an hour later when you returned to that spot during your patrol you wouldn't see anything there. Sure enough, if you then followed one of the known trails leading into Afghanistan you would see the blooms down there once again. We were watching potential Taleban and al-Qaeda fighters smoking their last cigarettes before they crossed the border. If we were able to find people crossing into Afghanistan we would let nearby Army or SOF teams know about it so that they could exploit this intelligence how best they saw fit. Sometimes they captured the fighters as they crossed the border, or sealed off the trail. We never fired on people crossing, as we had very strict ROE [Rules of Engagement] on who was a combatant and who was not.

'However, on 15 July 2005 I was orbiting over an outpost south of Khost, which was located right up against the Pakistani border. The US troops manning the FOB had been taking accurate 122 mm rocket fire and were getting pummelled. We were at about 15,000 ft above the FOB, which was barely the size of a football field. We could see rockets landing *inside* its perimeter, which meant that the enemy was pretty well dialed into the target.

'We definitely wanted to knock the rocket launchers out if we could find them. I just happened to be looking at a clearing about five miles

An A-10A from the 354th EFS takes off from Bagram AB on 10 October 2005 as maintainers prepare several other jets from the 'Bulldogs' for flight. In the foreground is 'the Dragon', the machine used to load and empty the ammunition drum of the A-10. It can empty spent shells and reload live ordnance in only 13 minutes *(USAF)*

from the FOB when I spotted several launchers situated across the border in Pakistan. Then, the ROE in OEF supported what I was about to do, stating that if anybody was actively shooting at US forces we were allowed to shoot back – even if someone was firing from across the border, or fled back across the border. As long as we were in definite pursuit we could go after them.

'Never taking my eyes off the launchers – if I did I knew I would never find them again – I pulled the jet toward the target. At a distance of about 2.5 miles I rolled in on the launchers – I had done this a million times in training, so I knew the timing, knew the cadence and knew about when I would be 6000 ft away from the impact area. My wingman never saw the target, despite me spending a considerable amount of time trying to talk his eyes onto the clearing, which was not much bigger than the size of a *7-ELEVEN* parking lot. He could not see what I was aiming at, so I told him to follow me, and he positioned himself about 4000-6000 ft behind me, and offset to the left.

'I rolled in in a pretty shallow dive – no more than 10-15 degrees – then rolled wings level, ready to strafe. I squeezed the trigger for about two seconds, then started my safe escape manoeuvre, turning away from the target area to avoid both being shot at and being fragged by my own bullets. My wingman then rolled in, and at about the time he was wings level I had already strafed and pulled off the target. The ground in front of him lit up as my rounds hit home, giving him a perfect aim point for his bullets. That was an old school strafing run – point and shoot. We put down more than 400 rounds of HEI, and follow-on forces who exploited the area counted 24 bodies.'

RUNWAY INCIDENTS

By late 2005, some three-and-a-half years after the initial A-10 unit had bedded down at Bagram, the runway at the base had seen very little in the way of improvement. However, efforts were at last being made to repair the entire length of the runway, thus making it better suited for heavy transports. Excessive use by the latter had routinely worn away spot patching in the runway undertaken by US military and civilian engineers. Flying into and out of Bagram, therefore, continued to be a contest of wills between pilots and the runway, and sometimes the runway won, as Maj Coggins related;

'The runway was made of 30-year-old concrete that had not been poured correctly in the first place. This meant that at any given time half of the 150 ft-wide runway was closed. Its first and last 1000 ft were full width, but the remaining 7000 ft was restricted to 75 ft only. When you were cleared for takeoff you would sit there for about four minutes in military power, and that allowed the motors to get fully up to operating temperature so that you would not have too much variation in them. Temperature variation caused the fan blades to change length, allowing air to bypass them and adversely affecting thrust levels. After four minutes of the engines spinning up to the right temperature, the lead A-10 was lined up on the open half of the runway, the pilot would release the brakes and the jet would takeoff on the 75 ft-wide section. The pilot of the second A-10 would throttle back, move over to the open side of the runway and immediately takeoff too.

'At night takeoffs were even tougher, as you would be wearing NVGs even for the taxi out to the runway. Afghanistan is unbelievably dark, with little ambient lighting, and to come home on NVGs to a 75 ft-wide runway was interesting to say the least. It was really a challenge to do the basics – takeoffs and landings – at Bagram'.

On 3 and 4 August 2005, Bagram had two runway incidents involving transport aircraft that closed the airfield. The first incident involved a C-130J that blocked the runway for several hours. This proved to be almost catastrophic for two A-10s that were returning to Bagram, as Lt Col Ken Craib, CO of the 74th EFS, explained;

'My wingman and I were returning after leading a rescue mission near Ghazni of a SOF team that was not transmitting. We had been given their intended route of march prior to takeoff, and my wingman and I were able to find them with the TGP. We marshalled some nearby ground forces who duly rescued the SOF team, and also effected a helicopter recovery of their wounded.

'We then headed back to Bagram, and just as we were approaching the base an air traffic controller told us that the runway had just been closed due to the C-130J incident. As the chief of wing safety I was needed on the ground to head up the investigation into the accident. Instead, I was stuck over the airfield unable to land. And to make matters worse, we were now starting to run low on gas and we had nowhere else to land. By this time the last tankers had already left Afghanistan, and the ASOC had to hastily turn one around that was over Tajikistan. Fortunately, the tanker got to us before we flamed out, having had to drop down pretty low to reach us. It then hung around after topping us off until the crews on the ground could get the Hercules off the runway.'

The following month the 74th EFS was replaced by the 354th EFS, which performed its third of four deployments to OEF in just four years between September 2005 and January 2006.

RENEWED FIGHTING

Arriving at Bagram in January, the cold weather and snow is the first thing personnel new to the country notice. However, for the 355th EFS, which arrived in-theatre in January 2006 to replace the 354th EFS, the weather at Bagram was a relief from the conditions blighting the unit's home at Eielson AFB, Alaska. On a typical January day, the temperature difference between Bagram and Eielson is a whopping 41°C, with the Alaskan base usually bottoming out at -26°C. One of the pilots to make the 2006 Bagram deployment with the 355th FS was first tour pilot 1Lt John Collier;

'Going from Eielson – a hardcore Arctic environment – to Bagram in the winter was not that much of a change of pace for us. However, the 354th FS guys from Tucson that we replaced said they had never been so cold in their lives, and they were telling us to bring electric blankets, goose down blankets and all this other stuff. When we got there from -40°C, we told them that Bagram was "kinda cold, but not really".'

When the 355th deployed to Bagram, expectations for a steady pace of weapons delivery were low, and the squadron's expectations were met. Winter is not the prime fighting season, with Taleban and al-Qaeda forces traditionally waiting the worst of the weather out before renewing combat in the spring. Despite the 'slowness', as one pilot described the deployment, 1Lt Collier did find himself involved in a situation where weapons were employed, but in a non-traditional manner;

'As the deployment neared its end, we had become used to not expending weapons. On this particular occasion we were sent down to the south of the country to work a high value target that was holed up in a building. The only other asset on station was a Predator, and no friendly forces were nearby. No sooner had we arrived than we received a 9-line target brief from the Predator controller and were cleared "hot". Being a young wingman, the speed at which this happened surprised me. As an A-10 guy, you are trained to check in with the JTAC on the radio, and you talk directly with him. If the JTAC has identified a target, or is coming under fire, then we know exactly what to do – attack. The tough part for us that day was that the lines of communication and who exactly was giving us approval to employ weapons were not exactly clear.

'When we checked in with the Predator we were not talking to the guy who was giving us clearance. We were talking to a UAV operator, who was in turn talking to the

Homicidal Hawg was the ladder door art carried by A-10A 79-0187 of the 355th EFS. It was also one of the very few A-10s to wear mission markings during its time at Bagram, this jet displaying six GBU-12 drops, one Mk 82 delivery and six strafing passes. The pilot's name is also displayed beneath the cockpit – the name bar is usually blank on A-10s during their time at Bagram *(Jack Behar)*

JTAC via mIRC-chat [military internet relay chat], who was e-mailing back to the Predator operator authorisation for us to employ ordnance on the building. Initially, we refused to drop, as our interpretation of the ROE at the time was this situation did not require CAS as there were no friendlies around. This tasking should have come from the CAOC, or have been directed by the CFACC. This was not CAS, and should have been scheduled in the daily Air Tasking Order as a TST.

'We explained to the UAV operator that there were no friendlies close to this building, yet he was telling us that CAS was required, and this had been approved by the JTAC he was in contact with. It was a very murky situation, but eventually we dropped an LGB on the building and destroyed it.

'As a result of this mission the squadron and the wing overhauled the procedures pertaining to A-10 operations with UAVs. I know the leadership in-theatre also had a big meeting about it. Our eyes had been opened to the command and control aspects of working with Predators, and clarification was needed in respect to who was giving the clearance for ordnance to be employed, how we met ROE and SPINS [Special Instructions] and who was establishing PID [Positive Identification]. A letter was subsequently issued to our pilots describing what had happened, clarifying how that mission, and situation, had met the intent of the ROE and the SPINS and why we had been cleared to employ the LGB. We had been thrown into a situation that we had not been trained for, or thought about. It was one of those things we had to work through in OEF as technology evolved.'

Often, the memorable missions were not those where ordnance was employed and the pilot brought the jet back 'Winchester', with all of its weapons expended. Rather, missions where more could have been done, and should have been done, linger the longest. Such was the case for 1Lt Collier during a late night XCAS (airborne alert CAS) flight, as he explained;

'We were sent over to an FOB near the Afghan-Pakistan border that had been taking some mortar fire, which was not uncommon for these outposts. It was late, about 0300 hrs, and we showed up over the FOB and start working the TGP. Within a few minutes we had spotted three

A-10A 80-0149, flown by Capt Nick DiCapua, poses for the camera behind a KC-135 on 26 March 2006. The jet is from the 355th FS at Eielson AFB, Alaska, the unit being in-theatre from January to May 2006. This would be the squadron's last deployment, as the 355th FS was deactivated in August 2007 following BRAC 2005 (USAF)

A-10A 80-0238 taxis onto the runway at Bagram on 15 May 2006. This mission would be the last for the 355th EFS at Bagram prior to it being relieved by the 81st EFS. It would also prove to be the squadron's last combat mission prior to deactivation *(Jack Behar)*

guys walking away from the FOB, right where the JTAC had told us to look. We didn't get to kill them, however, as there were some ROE and SPINS issues that needed to be resolved. By the time we got the approval to strafe them, they had reached a village and entered a hut – we had two TGPs on the hut, which was not connected to any other buildings. They walked out of there about ten minutes later, and we watched them cross the border into Pakistan. The ground commander was not comfortable with us putting 30 mm on them since there was a small chance that these three individuals were not the same ones that we had seen enter the hut.

'We always tried to err on the side of caution, and once this particular sortie was over we walked back into the squadron operations building at Bagram knowing that we should have been about to debrief a mission where we had employed ordnance and killed those guys. The JTAC had met all the required ROE, and when we got a chance to sit back and review the mission tapes from the TGPs, it seemed pretty obvious that we had eyes on the mortar operators. The outpost was in a very remote part of the country, these guys were out walking at 0300 hrs and we had just so happened to pick them up adjacent to where the mortar rounds had been fired from. I'll never forget letting those guys go. It was frustrating, and it pissed me off.'

'384th EFS' ARRIVES

The tasking for AEF 1/2 Cycle 6 at Bagram, which would take place during the summer of 2006, was for 14 A-10s. The 81st FS was the designated unit, the Spangdahlem-based fighter squadron making its third tour of Afghanistan. As had been the case the last time the unit operated from Bagram (in 2004-05), the 81st would be unable to independently support the deployment with 14 flyable airframes. Many of the A-10s belonging to the squadron had already reached 10,000 flying hours and been grounded. In mid-2005 it had been determined that after 10,000 hours the A-10 would need new wings. With a large number of the 81st's Primary Assigned Aircraft approaching that limit, the squadron would be unable to get 14 jets into a position to deploy and fly the high number of hours from Bagram that the OEF tasking required, and then return to Spangdahlem, all while remaining within the 10,000-hour limit.

Either an ANG or AFRes A-10 squadron would have to augment the 81st with both aircraft and personnel, and the 303rd FS was duly chosen to make its second OEF deployment – it had augmented the 706th FS in 2002. The 303rd would deploy six A-10A airframes and a group of pilots and maintainers.

Planning for the deployment began in December 2005, when senior officers from the 303rd FS flew to Spangdahlem to work out details with their counterparts in the 81st FS. Lt Col Keith McBride was the commanding officer of the latter unit, and he recalled;

'Usually when you take a unit into combat you have trained together to the same standard for a long time. Early on in the work-ups the pilots' personalities have usually come to the fore, and the leadership cadre uses this to match up individuals as flight leads and wingmen in combat pairs. Before we met the 303rd there was some concern that the reserve unit would try to act like a unit within a unit. And anytime you have an organisation working within another organisation the overall mission performance suffers. However, the December meeting convinced me that this would not be the case with the 303rd.

'The 81st FS was the lead unit for the deployment, and the reservists plainly stated that they were more than happy to be folded into our operation. Their commanding officer would be my deputy, while his DO would deploy as my No 3. We met the initial group of pilots from the 303rd for the first time on 10 May as our eight deploying A-10s flew from Germany to NAS Sigonella, Sicily, where we rendezvoused with the six AFRes airframes that had flown in from the USA via the Azores. The first group of pilots from Whiteman were a very experienced bunch, including eight instructor pilots, a flight lead and a single experienced wingman. That was great for us, as our squadron had a large number of junior pilots within its ranks. That first night when we all met up, we shared a big Italian dinner – pasta and wine – and introduced ourselves to each other.

'Two days later we departed for Afghanistan. We merged immediately after takeoff and flew in two five-ship formations and one four-ship. I took the first five-ship, with three jets from my squadron and two from the 303rd. We initially flew to Al Udeid air base, in Qatar, and then pressed on to Bagram.

'Another important step for us in the integration process was the unofficial re-designation of the squadron once in-theatre. We went from being the 81st EFS to the "384th EFS" by adding the numbers of the two component units together. Officially, of course, we remained the 81st EFS, but we reported to the whole theatre, including the CAOC, as the "384th EFS" – eventually, everyone referred to us as the "384th EFS" too. If you want to turn two camps into one you have to share some things, and sharing that designation helped a lot.'

As the '384th EFS' took over Bagram A-10 operations, things in Afghanistan were still relatively quiet – pretty much as they had been since *Anaconda* ended more than four years earlier. Operation *Mountain Lion* was coming to an end in the eastern part of the country and Operation *Mountain Thrust* was still in its infancy in southern Afghanistan. However, it would not be long before the A-10 pilots were supporting the largest number of CAS events and employing the greatest amount of ordnance since *Anaconda*.

Maintainers from the 303rd FS work to reload an A-10 with 30 mm HEI rounds. They are handling the plastic driving bands that guided the rounds and provide less wear and tear on the barrel, thus helping maintain the accuracy of the gun. The 30 mm shells are quite large, measuring 11.4 inches (290 mm) and weighing at least 1.53 lbs (0.69 kg) *(442nd FW)*

A maintainer pulls pins from a waiting A-10 at the EOR at Bagram AB, thus arming the ordnance just prior to takeoff. According to Capt David Raymond of the 81st EFS, 'The maintainers did a fantastic job. They were simply amazing. Thanks to their efforts we flew 100 per cent of our assigned tasks, which was a monumental feat' *(442nd FW)*

One of the newest pilots in the 81st FS was 1Lt David Kirkendall who was making his first combat deployment. Within three weeks of his arrival at Bagram he had dropped his first weapons and been part of a formation where his flight lead, Capt Scott Markle, would eventually be awarded the USAF's MacKay Trophy for the most meritorious flight of 2006. 1Lt Kirkendall recalled;

'On 2 June I flew my second mission in-theatre, with 303rd pilot Maj Tony Roe as my flight lead. He was a weapons officer, a pretty experienced pilot and a really smart guy. We took off to support an operation to the southwest, and by the time we arrived two of our A-10s were already on scene. They gave us the "high five" and showed us where everything was on the ground. We go to drop a couple of LGBs, and I was pretty psyched to have not messed anything up prior to returning to base. It was the most "vanilla" drop I had all summer, but it was a pretty good one to cut your teeth on.'

'That drop with 1Lt Kirkendall was memorable mostly because I hate to miss a target', explained Maj Roe. 'I had his target locked up and ready to go when I then heard some garbled communications and thought that he was telling me he was off "dry", without having dropped his LGB. I turned off my laser, which caused his bomb to fall short of the intended target due to my screw up. He did a great job lasing my bomb in on my pass, however!'

Two weeks later, on 16 June, 1Lt Kirkendall was flying with 81st FS pilot Capt Scott Markle as his flight lead. Taking off just before dawn, the two A-10 pilots were supposed to fly to a location near Kandahar, but almost immediately things changed and they were moved to a TIC near the village of Orgun-E on the Afghan-Pakistani border. A 15-member SOF team had been ambushed by a larger force of Taleban fighters, and they were now in desperate need of CAS as 1Lt Kirkendall recalled;

'We showed up just as all the other assets had been pulled, including an AC-130 that had to leave before the sun came up. The SOF team was not expecting any further contact, but it got pinned down by heavy machine gun fire in a valley at sunrise. This was a bad time of day for us to mount an effective aerial attack because the sun was at such an angle it was difficult to see the ground. Nevertheless, Capt Markle was able to figure out where the SOF team was taking fire from. The problem was that some of the friendlies were involved in hand-to-hand with the Taleban – they were right on top of each other. Capt Markle flew a really low pass and dropped some flares, one of which landed very close to the SOF guys. The flares momentarily halted the enemy fire, allowing the friendlies to separate themselves from the Taleban.

'The enemy had three machine gun nests targeting the SOF team, and we ended up firing 30 mm cannon rounds within 30 m of the friendlies.

The seven-round LAU-131/A rocket pod was used extensively by A-10As in OEF, with at least one launcher carried on each aircraft. The primary weapon fired from the store was the WP target marking round, which allowed A-10 pilots to pinpoint targets prior to engaging them with larger weapons *(Capt Tom Harney)*

That was very close – half the distance we normally call "danger close", which is usually our minimum. We were able to make seven or eight passes each, firing more than 2000 rounds in total that allowed the SOF team to move 300 m away from the Taleban. Capt Markle then rolled in and dropped a Mk 82 airburst on the machine guns, but the bomb did not fuse and the machine guns continued to fire at the SOF team. He repositioned and fired off a WP rocket at the machine guns, and I rolled in and put down a Mk 82 through the smoke of his WP. That bomb did fuse and the machine gun fire immediately stopped.

'For the rest of the day, a lot of air power was focused on that area, pretty much levelling the hill on which the machine gun nests were sited. All the SOF guys got out alive, although a few were wounded, but no one was killed – sadly, that was not always the case when we provided CAS during the deadly summer of 2006.'

Capt Markle and 1Lt Kirkendall were credited with destroying all three machine gun nests and killing 40 enemy combatants during the engagement.

Two A-10s from the 81st EFS taxi out at Bagram AB on 12 June 2006 at the start of yet another mission in support of ISAF forces. While A-10s usually flew in pairs in-theatre, there was pressure to fly single-ship missions, as 81st FS CO Lt Col Keith McBride recalled. 'I refused to fly single-ship missions, despite HQ wanting us to split up our assets to cover more area when the Taleban offensive increased in ferocity. The army was always requesting more coverage, and one of the solutions it came up with was to spilt up formations and send single ships over northwestern Afghanistan. I refused to go along with this, however. When we were pressed hard about it, I explained to our leadership that in those western areas where they wanted the A-10s we had no way of monitoring where our jets were. Sure, the pilots might be talking to a JTAC who had SATCOM back to his ops centre. However, as far as we were concerned we had no way to monitor where our guys were. If the single-ship suffered a malfunction and the pilot had to eject, we would have had no idea that this had happened until he failed to report back to base when his patrol ended some three hours later' *(USAF)*

'I was quite nervous about making strafing runs', explained 1Lt Kirkendall. 'To give you an idea of how close we were shooting, looking through the gun cross in the HUD, the centre was where the enemy was and one mark over was where the friendlies were. We actually got to talk to the SOF guys after the action had ended, and they told us that they were scrambling for cover, trying to get behind trees, as our cannon rounds were kicking up rocks and dirt in their direction as they hit the ground. A lot was going on and there was not a lot of time to think about it, and that is when your training really comes to the fore.'

OPERATION *MOUNTAIN THRUST*

The battle for southern Afghanistan began in the spring of 2006 when a resurgent Taleban emerged from the winter with a renewed energy to fight American, Afghan and Coalition forces. Taleban and foreign fighters infiltrated the southern provinces of the country, taking over villages and ramping up attacks on Afghan and Coalition forces. Evidence of Taleban control was the public execution of a man accused of murder in the city of Gizab, in the province of Uruzgan. The execution demonstrated to the local population, and the international community, just how much power the Taleban had in the province in respect to the group's ability to enforce the laws they had originally established whilst ruling the country.

Operation *Mountain Lion* in Kunar Province had worked to push the Taleban out of eastern Afghanistan, but a larger offensive was needed to combat them in the south, where their presence was at its strongest and resistance would be fierce. Pacification of contested areas and disruption of supply routes from Pakistan were to be the objectives of *Mountain Thrust*, paving the way for the International Security Assistance Force (ISAF) to

initiate Stage III of its expansion. Several months earlier, on 8 December 2005 during a meeting at NATO Headquarters in Brussels, the Foreign Ministers of the NATO member countries had approved ISAF's extension of control to the south. The handover of power from US military control to ISAF control would occur on 31 July 2006 in Kandahar. The Coalition was keen for a successful transition, and it knew that the key to achieving this was a major offensive to eliminate, or reduce, the Taleban presence and control in the provinces of Helmand and Uruzgan.

The initial phase of this campaign commenced on 15 May 2006 under the control of CJTF-76 when Coalition Special Forces infiltrated the targeted provinces in preparation for the launch of *Mountain Thrust*, which was scheduled to take place on 14 June. In late May, a five-man patrol of Australian SAS accompanied by an American JTAC from the USAF's Special Tactics Squadrons departed the Australian base of operations in Tarin Kowt (the capital of Uruzgan Province) in order to establish an observation post near the Chora Pass, about 30 km northeast of their base. Late in the afternoon of 2 June the patrol found that its position had been compromised, and it began to face overwhelming odds as a large Taleban force ascended towards its position. Enemy snipers from an opposite peak eliminated their option for disengagement, so the only choice left open to them was to stand and fight – and call for CAS.

Taking off from Bagram that afternoon, Lt Col McBride and his wingman, 1Lt Tim Manning, headed for a pre-fragged target about 300 miles from Bagram that would take them an hour to reach. 'Shortly after takeoff, we got diverted to a TIC situation by the controlling agency', explained Lt Col McBride. 'I quickly plotted it on the map and figured out that the TIC was just 25 miles away. I got my wingman ready to go by performing a quick systems check, talking him through a fire-to-fire plan and briefing him on where we were headed and what we were going to do. That took about three minutes to complete. I then switched over to contact the JTAC on the spot, call sign "Jaguar". I soon made radio contact with him as I headed in their direction. Whilst travelling at about five miles a minute, the JTAC and I very calmly performed our back and forth authentication, after which he asked me "How far out are you?" I told him five minutes. He replied "That will be just about right".

'As we were heading inbound my Litening pod malfunctioned, its sensor spinning around uselessly. 1Lt Manning was a pretty young wingman, so I put him in high trail. We arrived on the scene just as the sun was going down, and I quickly identified which hill the SAS team was on. I also spotted a nearby village, and I knew that the approaching Taleban had come from here. In the subdued light at dusk, however, I couldn't see them. I had to rely on the JTAC to tell me where they were in relation to his position. As I rolled in the JTAC gave me clearance to expend a weapon. I threw a Mk 82 airburst at a hillside some way from the SAS team and somewhere near where I thought the Taleban were approaching from. Although it was not an accurate drop, missing the enemy by 400 m, it certainly got their attention and they stopped moving up the hill. They instead chose to hunker down where they were and continue to fire up at the Aussies and the JTAC.

'We then tried to get the bombs closer to where these guys were on the hill. Having achieved this, I wanted to throw down some rockets to mark their position. So I rolled in and tried to shoot a WP but it didn't work. I repeated my attack and again the rocket failed to fire. I made one more pass and this time a rocket did indeed hit the target area. The fourth one I tried failed, however. These duds stymied my efforts to drop additional weapons on the enemy. Early on in the deployment we had been plagued by malfunctioning rockets due to all the dust we had to deal with at Bagram. We were trying to use the WP so that the JTAC could move us as required onto the enemy.

'Despite our ordnance problems, we still managed to get the insurgents on the side of the hill to start moving back down towards the village. We kept on circling around the hill as the sun went down, happy in the knowledge that the Taleban were now having trouble seeing us. Once it was completely dark we would turn all of our internal and external lights off and switch to NVGs, but we were not quite there yet as it was still dusk.

'As the main body of insurgents moved back to the village, they left behind a handful of fighters manning some heavy machine guns that were still firing, and the JTAC wanted us to strafe them. We rolled in and strafed these targets using low-angle gunnery passes that varied in height from 300-800 ft above the ground. I had to get close to the guns in order to ascertain where these guys were as it was now getting darker. We made a series of low-angle strafing passes, climbing back up over the top of the hill and then circling around the other side to repeat the attack. I was using the hill the Aussies were on as a barrier so that we could climb up and not get shot at by the people we were shooting at. We did that for a while, but it eventually got too dark to safely make strafing runs. So we climbed up and put our NVGs on.

'The threat to the SOF team was not as great as it had previously been, but the snipers were still posing a problem. I asked the JTAC to use his IR laser marker to point out where they were on the opposite hill, but he radioed back to tell me that the batteries in his pointer were dead. I decided to use the pointer in my TGP instead, telling the JTAC that I would point it from my cockpit at his position and then move it away until he told me when to stop once it had located one of the snipers. I would then know where to shoot. This plan was abandoned when he told me that his NVGs had been destroyed during the recent firefight. The only remaining option

Capt Rick Mitchell makes final cockpit checks before taxiing for takeoff at Bagram AB in A-10A 81-0945 in August 2006. Capt Mitchell was a reservist from the 303rd FS, and part of that unit's contribution to the 81st EFS. He is wearing NVGs, which are an incredible aid to pilots at night but are by no means perfect, reducing field-of-view to around 40 degrees. This can in turn create issues with spatial disorientation (USAF)

was for him to identify his location with an IR marker so that I could start strafing east of his position, and he could then move me either east or west of that spot onto the snipers. What I wanted to do was to shoot as close to the friendlies as I safely could then keep moving away from their position towards the enemy.

'Just as we were getting ready to do this the JTAC told me that he couldn't see us at all, and requested that we turn our lights on. Once we had done this our A-10s looked like the Starship Enterprise! At least he could now see us, and knowing which way our noses were pointing, he knew we weren't going to shoot him. The aiming reticule was at about 50 millirads, which was about three degrees, and we knew that the bullet dispersion would be well inside of that. I then briefed my very inexperienced wingman on what we were going to do. On our first pass we were going to put the SOF team's IR marker outside of the aiming reference and then aim at the top of the hill, which we could easily see through our NVGs. The JTAC would then talk us in from those initial impact points to where the snipers were.

'I rolled in, with all my lights on, and got a very late clearance to fire from the JTAC, as we were going to be shooting very close to him. He was a bit nervous, and he ended up waiting until the last moment to clear me "hot". I only managed to fire a few rounds before I pulled off the target – not a lot, but enough for 1Lt Manning to see my aiming point. As he rolled in behind me, the JTAC told him to shoot 20 m east of my impacts. This was a little further away from the SOF team, so I was comfortable with that. As I made my recovery and turned away, I looked over my shoulder to see him strafing. He got a really long pull on the trigger, which was good because we didn't have a precise location for the snipers and we wanted to cover as large an area as possible with a decent number of rounds to provide weapons effects.

'As 1Lt Manning started to pull off I could see his shells initially impacting where mine had hit and then start to move off to the left. As he fired the gun he stood on the rudder and moved the weapon to the left. This got me very worried as I could see the bullets running down the ridge perpendicular to his flightpath. I knew that when he let go of the rudder the nose of the A-10 was going to snap back the other way, the jet typically overcorrecting in the opposite direction. If he still had his finger on the trigger when he let go of the rudder the bullets would track back into the friendly position. I need not have been concerned, however, as 1Lt Manning let go of the trigger before he let go of the rudder. Indeed, he made a pretty devastating strafing pass on the hill. We followed up with a few more strafing runs in order to eliminate the sniper threat, then handed the tasking over to another pair of A-10s and headed back to base.'

Summer at Bagram was not without its challenges for the '384th EFS'. The low-density altitude of the airfield limited the amount of weapons the A-10 could carry due to the simple fact that the jet would not take off from Bagram carrying a full load of ordnance. The squadron experimented with numerous options to work around this issue, including reducing the amount of fuel that was carried on departure provided a tanker was available nearby. One of the limitations initially imposed on the pilots was departing Bagram with the jet's magazine only half-loaded. 'You soon learned to hold a few rounds in reserve for the JTAC in case things went bad', 1Lt Kirkendall explained. Eventually permission was granted towards the end of the deployment for a full gun load on takeoff.

Fighting between ISAF and insurgent forces only intensified as the summer of 2006 wore on, and the pace of operations for the '384th EFS' increased month on month and the flying hours rapidly built up. This was principally because of the ceaseless demand for CAS from troops who were engaged by large numbers of Taleban fighters. There was also a lack of understanding by controlling authorities within ISAF that the A-10 pilots at Bagram were close to being tasked beyond their safe levels of endurance.

On his second deployment to Bagram in 2006, Lt Col Brian Borgen was the 303rd's deputy commanding officer. He explained the situation facing the '384th' as follows;

'When you went to the bombing range to train for an OEF deployment you would start out with a simple planned mission, which would progress into a more volatile situation and culminate in the dreaded TIC call. During the summer of 2006, it felt as if every single sortie culminated in a TIC situation. Often, there would be two or three TICs for us to have to deal with during the course of just one sortie. The missions also became extremely long, as we didn't have a good handle – and neither did the ASOC – on when to pull guys out of the fight and send them home. You would launch on a 4.5-hour sortie and often stay aloft for five, six or seven hours. We would be sent TIC after TIC as long as we could still get gas and had ordnance hanging on the jet.

'The "Hog" had more than proven its worth over Afghanistan since March 2002, being quick to answer the CAS call and well suited to supporting TIC. However, in terms of numbers in-theatre, it was a minimal asset that was struggling to cope with the ASOC's maximum need. It was believed, erroneously, that the way to get more out of the A-10 was to keep people up there on station for longer periods. This meant that the "384th" was operating at maximum sustainable rate, and if you added all those unplanned hours onto each planned sortie, you were looking at serious problems for the jets' maintenance phase line further down the road.'

It was not easy striking a balance between keeping aircraft available on the flightline and making sure that maintenance crews got to service the 14 A-10s flown by the '384th'. Ultimately, thanks to the outstanding work performed by the maintainers from both the 81st and 303rd, the squadron was able to fulfil 100 per cent of its assigned taskings and never refused a sortie because it did not have an aeroplane available.

'With the 14 A-10s we had, at any one time there was one in phase maintenance, where all the covers were taken off and all the wires and cables inspected to make sure everything was still working', recalled Lt Col McBride. 'Despite the fact that we were flying a huge number of sorties, we had to periodically ground aircraft for up to two weeks at a time so that their scheduled phase inspection – due every 500 flying hours – could be carried out. Add to this the one or two aircraft that pilots had reported as "broken" from their previous flights, and now we were down three jets from our original strength of 14. We had to have three fully serviceable A-10s on alert at all times – two primaries and one spare – and all of a sudden we were down to eight jets for planned sorties.

'Anytime we had two pilots stepping out to the flightline we needed to have a spare available in case one of their assigned jets failed to launch. Instead of waiting around for an hour while maintenance tried to fix it, the pilot would simply switch to the spare. We tried to fly six jets for the 16 mission slots we were assigned each day, with two aircraft as spares. Each of our serviceable A-10s would fly about three times a day during the deployment.'

The presence of UAVs over the battlespace continued to grow, and the interoperability of manned and unmanned aircraft, though at times rough and riddled with uncertainty, was quickly apparent. With a superior

The rugged terrain that covers much of Afghanistan forms a dramatic backdrop for this 303rd FS jet on patrol during the summer of 2006. Finding targets in the mountains and valleys has been one of the greatest challenges facing Coalition air power in OEF *(Maj David Kirkendall)*

sensor to the A-10's TGP, the Predator's ability to find and track targets permitted a successful engagement on numerous occasions. One mission flown by Lt Col Borgen illustrated the growing ability of the two platforms to collaborate in OEF;

'We were down south conducting an overwatch mission on the lookout for a sniper who had been working over our guys for several days. His firing position was within a village, and the friendlies struggled to isolate him until they received the assistance of a Predator. They targeted the sniper's building within the village and chased him out into the open. As he started running across an open field we moved in and began working with the Predator, whose sensor had the sniper locked up. As I could not see him with the naked eye or with my pod, I asked the Predator to lase the guy. I then used my jet's laser spot tracker to lock onto his position via my Litening pod. The JTAC gave me clearance to fire and I strafed on that spot, without ever physically seeing my target.

'Taking out a solitary figure running across an open field in an A-10 was something that we could never have done without the targeting pod and its laser capability, and integrating this with other assets. Although the eradication of a single sniper was somewhat anti-climactic when compared to taking out a whole group of bad guys, it clearly illustrated the pinpoint accuracy of the technology that had been added to what was a 30-year-old aeroplane.'

One of the most exceptional things to emerge from the deployment was the relationship that developed between the '384th EFS' and the Special Tactics Squadrons (STSs) that were based at Bagram. Their

Senior Airman Adam Servais was a USAF combat controller who was assigned to the 23rd STS at Bagram when he was killed calling in air support during an ambush near Tarin Kowt, in the Uruzgan Province, on 19 August 2006. The 81st EFS developed a special relationship with the 23rd STS and its controllers, working almost daily with them, either planning an operation or providing CAS. For Capt David Raymond, the loss of Servais was particularly sobering. 'It hit us all pretty hard because we all knew him, and many of us had had conversations with him. He employed our aircraft dozens of times and then he died during our deployment. I talked to his team leader and expressed my condolences, and he replied "We have got a job to do. He is dead so let it go. Get ready for tomorrow's mission". That kind of hit home. I developed a greater sense and idea of what we do as CAS pilots following Servais' loss, and I tried to impart this to my squadronmates on a daily basis from then on' *(USAF)*

An enlisted combat controller works a ROVER system, enabling him to see what the pilot's targeting pod was looking at. The Remote Operational Video Enhanced Receiver was developed in early 2002, but it was initially too large to be carried. The system was eventually reduced to the size of a laptop, and its employment dramatically reduced the time for, and accuracy of, CAS missions *(USAF)*

operations centre was just 100 m from the '384th's', and a close relationship quickly developed between the units. Pilots would interact with the STS airmen face to face when they were at Bagram, and then talk to them over the radio when they were in the field requesting CAS. By heading down to the STS operations centre after hearing the radios 'light up' with traffic or seeing TIC-related communications come across the 'classified chat', pilots could get a better sense of how the fight was shaping. The '384th's' flying supervisor could immediately find out about any TIC situation, ascertaining whether the A-10s could expect a long, tough fight or begin to take precautionary measures. This relationship allowed the STS and the aircraft supporting them to work from the same game plan.

'In late July I got to work with an STS JTAC', Lt Col McBride recalled. 'He was with a SOF team that was watching a section of road along which a convoy was due to pass the next morning. They had watched some guys plant an IED in this road and then move to a nearby building. One of them had subsequently walked outside to a nearby treeline and made a call on a cell phone. We arrived overhead and got a fix on the building and the guy in the treeline. The JTAC wanted one of us to strafe the treeline and the second jet to drop a bomb on the building. My wingman and I quickly set up for our run in. I was going to strafe the treeline and my wingman would bomb the building.

'The JTAC gave us clearance to employ ordnance, and I rolled in and fired my gun at the treeline. However, instead of dropping his bomb, my wingman came off dry due to a switch error. So, following my strafing pass and the abortive bombing run, 41 more guys came streaming out of the building and started heading in every direction, spilling into nearby fields and into the treelines. The JTAC had a ROVER [Remote Operational Video Enhanced Receiver], and with my TGP we then spent the next 50 minutes hunting down and killing all 41 of those guys. You could only have done that with a targeting pod, as the naked eye or NVGs were useless for picking up individuals from the heights were operating at in Afghanistan.

'Using the ROVER, the JTAC would tell me to head across the road into a specific field, as he could see five guys running through there. So, I slewed my TGP across the road and into the field, expanding its field of view. The JTAC told me to move it north a bit, which I did, and I then zoomed in. Sure enough, there were five guys hiding behind a row of bushes. Now we could go and drop them.

'Working with the JTAC, we were able to decide which type of ordnance would be the best to employ in this situation. With guys hiding in a cultivated field, lying down between furrows, the Mk 82 airburst was the weapon of choice. The gun ran the bomb a close second, as the 30 mm HEI rounds had to land pretty close to the target because they were only one-third the size of a hand grenade. With either the Mk 82 or the gun, you needed a number of enemy combatants huddled together if you were going to get the weapons effect on a human that you were looking for. And if we hadn't have had that targeting pod all 41 of these guys would have escaped.

'We saved our two LGBs and took them back up to where the IED had been planted in the road. It was easy to see the spot where the enemy had been digging through the TGP, as the dirt they had just unearthed was a different temperature to everything around it. We dropped our LGBs on the IED and got a secondary explosion. Hopefully, we had completely destroyed it, but at the very least we marked the IED's location well enough for EOD [Explosive Ordnance Disposal] to find it.'

'86 CLEARED HOT'

Over Helmand Province in the southwest of Afghanistan, one particular 30-mile x 30-mile kill box had been nicknamed '86CH'. Within this kill

Nighttime did not slow down the pace of operations for the A-10A thanks to NVGs, the SUU-25 IR flare dispenser and the Litening targeting pod. The latter system was the game changer for nocturnal operations, allowing the 'Hog' to be as lethal at night as it was during the hours of daylight *(USAF)*

box were the towns of Sangin and Musa Qala, as well as the Kajaki Dam. '86CH' had remained unvisited by A-10s of the '384th EFS' until 25 June 2006. However, from then on the area was routinely patrolled by the squadron, with ordnance being consistently employed there. Indeed, the pilots began calling the kill box '86 Cleared Hot', as someone was always there clearing them to attack the enemy.

Capt Matthew Robins and 1Lt Jay Pease were scheduled to fly on a standard XCAS night mission, but the summer thunderstorm activity was so severe that their flight was cancelled prior to them briefing for it. However, even though they expected to remain firmly on the ground, the pilots decided to brief their mission. Whilst working out the specifics of the original XCAS sortie they were given a new mission to perform, as Capt Robins explained;

'They threw some coordinates at us and we plotted them out. Sure enough, they were right on the border with Pakistan. Attacking such targets in this area was always a risky business, particularly at night. If you strayed onto the wrong side of the border there would be Hell to pay. It was always pretty difficult to tell where Afghanistan ended and Pakistan began, so you generally tried to stay as far away from this area as you possibly could.

'We took off at around midnight, and en route to the target area it became clear that the entire eastern border was covered with very active thunderstorm cells. Once we actually made contact with the JTAC on the ground, he had several tasks for us, all of which were under the weather. I directed 1Lt Pease to hold high while I took a look, all the while thinking to myself that this was the worst place in the world to be in an aeroplane – stuck between thunderclouds in the mountains at night. Fortunately, we were soon re-tasked by the ASOC. Having refuelled from a tanker, we had just started to work the second tasking when we got a new call. We were already three hours into a sortie on a night that was supposed to

Lt Col Keith McBride departs Bagram AB in A-10A 78-0631 on 4 July 2006 to begin a CAS mission in support of OEF. Lt Col McBride was the commanding officer of the 81st EFS during the squadron's 2006 deployment *(442nd FW)*

be a wash out, and we were 250 miles from Bagram. The call sent us even further south, to the town of Sangin.

'On the way we tried to piece together what was going on. There was a foot patrol that had pushed a little too deeply into virtually uncontested Taleban territory, but the ASOC wouldn't really tell us what was going on – it was one of those missions. I had 1Lt Pease climb up into a high block position so that we could collect SA by simply watching what was happening on the ground through the TGP and listening to the radio chatter. We eventually found out that there was a foot patrol way out in the "boonies", and a ground convoy of mostly ANA [Afghan National Army] and some SOF guys were on their way to pick them up. I was totally unfamiliar with the territory and it was still dark, but at least the cloud cover had cleared up.

'The convoy – which had no air-to-ground communication capability – radioed back to its FOB to ask us for a show of force. It was approaching a residential area, and the troops wanted to pound their chests a bit, just in case. We got visual on the convoy, did the show of force and then all Hell broke loose. We learned later that immediately following the show of force, the Morning Prayer call was broadcast over the loudspeakers in the village – but it wasn't prayer time just yet. That was a call for volunteers to take up weapons and engage the convoy!

'Within minutes the ANA and SOF troops were being targeted by accurate RPG and heavy machine gun [HMG] fire, which 1Lt Pease could see from his high block position. But we still couldn't break the communication chain from us to the FOB and on to the ground convoy to get clearance to shoot. Rather, the convoy opted for danger-close 105 mm rounds from artillery pieces within the FOB. The convoy commander felt that was the safer option since he still couldn't locate the missing foot patrol. We began spotting for the artillery, trying to walk the shells in towards the convoy's attackers.

'While spotting for the artillery, I located the foot patrol, struggling through its own barrage of RPG and HMG fire, about two miles away. Since the convoy didn't know we were visual with both sets of friendlies, we were held high for several minutes. Once I convinced the JTAC at the FOB that I could see all the friendlies, we finally got our first 9-line briefs for targets to attack. Before long we were shooting just outside of danger-close range into the HMG firing positions that were engaging the now stranded convoy.

'By this time we were getting low on gas, and 1Lt Pease began coordinating a tanker for us. He surprised me with his ingenuity – the tanker showed up overhead the firefight, so we could just pop up, get enough gas to stay above bingo fuel and then dive back into the action, rather than having a 30-minute round trip.

'This mission took place in the height of summer, which meant that we could only launch with half a magazine load of ammunition because of limited takeoff performance at Bagram. After our third or fourth pass I started to get antsy about ammo rationing, and asked the JTAC if we could switch to WP instead to at least keep the enemies' heads down while preserving some actual stopping power just in case it was required. The bombs we were carrying were pretty useless in this situation as we were just too close to the friendlies for them to be employed safely.

The pilot of A-10A 81-0963 sits off the starboard wingtip of a KC-135R after having the jet's tanks topped off mid-mission. This aircraft was destroyed in a non-fatal flying accident near Laufeld, Germany, on 1 April 2011 (442nd FW)

'As the sun was coming up, about 5.5 hours into the mission, we finally made direct contact with a JTAC that was assigned to the foot patrol. He informed us they'd been taking heavy fire from multiple locations, and then began passing us 9-line briefs. The JTAC at the FOB let him take over, and we started strafing targets in support of the foot patrol. At no time did the convoy or foot patrol ever have direct radio contact with each other. It was all relayed back through the FOB.

'After one or two gun runs and some WPs to help protect the foot patrol manoeuvre, things took a turn for the worst. It was now fully daylight, the foot patrol had gotten itself pinned down, I had lost visual contact with the friendlies and I couldn't see the origination of the HMG sites anymore. I elected to put 1Lt Pease in a trail formation and fly low over the area, hoping to get at least a tally on any muzzle flashes shooting at us. While our pass wasn't very successful, it did manage to give the JTAC just enough time to create the best 9-line brief I've ever received over the radio. He passed us coordinates for a target building that was the source of most of the fire they were taking. He cited it as being 100 m away. No problem, as danger-close for us was 65 m. He talked us onto the target, and told us that the foot patrol was now all under cover. In fact, he and the troops were lying in a ditch that was coming under a hail of fire. I'll never know how he managed to build that 9-line with spot-on coordinates.

'Unbeknownst to any of us, the ground convoy commander had taken it upon himself to charge the area in an attempt to rescue the foot patrol. I had only 90 rounds of 30 mm ammunition left and my wingman had about 200 rounds. As we would be approaching bingo fuel immediately after the strafing run, I told 1Lt Pease to let them have all the ammunition he had left. I rolled in and hit the building, and as I pulled off my wingman did just what I had asked of him. By the time he had finished his run

1Lt Pease had made the building look like we had dropped a bomb on it after all. I'm sure the convoy commander thought so too, as he was only 300 m away when the building was hit by a wall of 30 mm rounds.

'At this point the JTAC from the FOB saw us strafing close to both sets of friendlies and called for an immediate "Ceasefire!" I had never been in that situation before, and it was the worst feeling ever. And we had lost contact with the JTAC in the foot patrol. We briefed the Harrier II flight that showed up to relieve us and then made the hour-long flight back to base. It was a depressing end to an eight-hour sortie. When we got back to Bagram things just got worse. Intel told us a CSAR had commenced for some missing guys in the same area. I was convinced that we had inadvertently shot too close to the foot patrol. Maybe they hadn't wanted the building struck on that side?

'The following day 1Lt Pease and I were invited down to Kabul to meet the guys we had been supporting, and there we were told the rest of the story. They had made it out after all.

'After our last pass, which was more like 15-20 m from the friendlies, rather than 100 m, the foot patrol had broken contact with the Taleban and effected a link up with the ground convoy. During their struggle to do so, and the chaos caused by having more than 200 rounds of 30 mm HEI impact 20 m away, the JTAC had dropped his radio into a water-filled ditch – that explained why we had lost contact. The FOB JTAC had called "Ceasefire" mainly because he knew that the friendlies were just 20 m from the building, not 100 m as the JTAC had told us. Shrapnel and building debris showering the foot patrol had tripped the

Pilots and groundcrew from the 303rd FS's contribution to the 81st EFS pose for a group photo in front of, and on, A-10A 78-0605 on 20 June 2006 *(442nd FW)*

Decorated by ordnancemen of the 303rd FS who were attached to the 81st EFS at Bagram in the summer of 2006, this 500-lb Mk 82 airburst bomb has been adorned with a Budweiser beer 'label' *(442nd FW)*

FOB JTAC's safety threshold and prompted him to call for a ceasefire. The JTAC in the ditch told us that he and his comrades had only managed to get out alive because the building's occupants had been neutralised. The enemy had HMGs sticking out of every window, but the 30 mm rounds easily pierced the building's stick ceiling and eradicated the Taleban threat.

'It was also heartbreaking to learn that the foot patrol had lost two of its own earlier that night, these men perishing in action during the scramble to link back up. This was prior to the JTAC having voice contact with the FOB, the ground convoy or air support. It was for those two fallen soldiers that the CSAR had been called, their bodies being successfully retrieved. The patrol was in the process of delivering their fallen comrades home when they had taken the opportunity to meet with the A-10 pilots who'd helped them out. I still maintain contact with the foot patrol JTAC, and will always wish that we'd somehow managed to effectively communicate that we were "visual, tally!" and effected CAS earlier, rather than merely aiding artillery spotting and making jet noise.'

Capt Robins was awarded an Air Medal with Valor and received the Order of Daedalians Exceptional Pilot Award for 2007 for this mission.

OPERATION *MEDUSA*

Continuing the push for control of southern Afghanistan, Operation *Medusa* was launched on 2 September 2006. The Canadian-led action would be NATO's first offensive ground operation, and Canada's largest military engagement since the Korean War. *Medusa* was designed to push Coalition forces back into the Kandahar area in another attempt to deny

A-10A 82-0649 was one of eight 'Hogs' sent to Bagram by the 81st FS to join the six A-10s committed by the 303rd FS. Officially, the unit was known as the 81st EFS, but unofficially the squadron assumed the title of the '384th EFS' by adding the numbers of the two squadrons together to form one new unit! By the end of the deployment even the CAOC had begun to refer to unit as the '384th EFS' *(442nd FW)*

areas of sanctuary for Taleban fighters, focusing on the Panjwai district where hundreds, and possibly thousands, of Taleban had assembled. Panjwai was the spiritual home of the Taleban, being the location where the movement began and the birthplace of the Taleban leader, Mullah Mohammed Omar. The Panjwai district, and its three primary villages of Panjwai, Zhari and Pashmul, also bordered Highway One, which was a vital link that connected Kandahar with Herat.

From early July through to early August, during Operation *Mountain Thrust*, Canadian troops had fought the first Battle of Panjwai, suffering four soldiers killed. This offensive had delayed Taleban plans to terrorise Kandahar. Now, a month later, the Taleban had returned.

During the second night of *Medusa* Capt David Raymond was flying with Col James Mackey of the 303rd FS. The two A-10 pilots were orbiting over an adjacent kill box north of *Medusa*, some 30 miles from the centre of the operation, waiting for a call to provide assistance. Capt Raymond explained what happened next;

'Looking south from our orbit, I could see a lot of firepower and explosions going off. At night it is really easy to spot a firefight as our

74

NVGs intensify any kind of light. I started to listen to the "freq" being used by the Canadian unit running the operation to see what was going on. They had an AC-130 gunship, a pair of A-10s, two Hornets and a Predator employing in the area. There were three JTACs working within 1.5 miles of each other in a target area that was just three nautical miles by three nautical miles in size. The result was total confusion, with a lot of talk on the radio and three guys asking for firepower. There was no coordination between any of the JTACs, and it seemed to me that they were treating their own particular area as an isolated battlespace, without considering that there were a lot of aeroplanes overhead.

'I got on the radio and spoke to one of the JTACs, telling him that I was 30 miles away and had two A-10s with plenty of ordnance and gas. As a qualified FAC(A) I explained that I could help him coordinate and "rack and stack" the aircraft overhead so that nobody ran into each other. He liked the idea and moved us in closer, but he told us that he was not going to use us to employ ordnance as we were not tasked to him. If I could get all the aircraft on the same "sheet of music" that would be a great help to the embattled JTAC.

'So I went ahead and did just that. He gave me the stack and I divided up the AO and quickly had all three JTACs on the same "freq" so that we could get a game plan going. With all this in place, I soon had the airspace divided up appropriately, and there was simultaneous weapon employment by an AC-130, the A-10s and Hornets and a kinetic Predator. I did this for a while, and ended up with about 12 minutes of fuel left before Col Mackey and I had to head back to Bagram. I asked the JTAC "pretty please if you don't mind" I would like to release my ordnance as there were a lot of targets that still needed servicing. So, he got on the radio and called the ASOC requesting permission for me to employ. This was granted and he assigned Col Mack and myself five targets.

'In doing so, the JTAC gave me dedicated control of the Canadian artillery that was supporting *Medusa*. We had always heard about artillery when honing our tactics in the A-10 during peacetime, and once in combat we always asked if we could use artillery if it was available. However, the ground commander usually had reasons why he did not want us to control it. That night I was given six "tubes" of M777 155 mm artillery to work with, which came as a total surprise to me. I asked the JTAC to label the targets that he had for me "1" through "5", and I would in turn let him know which target was going to get what ordnance. I asked for Type 3 control of the target.'

Type 3 control is used when the JTAC is providing clearance for multiple attacks within a single engagement, and one or all of the following conditions exist – the JTAC is either unable to visually acquire the attacking aircraft at weapons release; the JTAC is unable to visually acquire the target; or the attacking aircraft is unable to acquire the mark-for-target prior to employing weapons.

Lt Col Raymond continued;

'I asked if the artillery had variable-time [VT] fused rounds, which were airburst rounds. We did not want to rely on a target talk-on from the JTAC, as we were really low on gas and wanted to do this quickly. Timely and effective ordnance was the name of the game. The JTAC gave me six tubes with VT rounds to work with. I directed the artillery to fire on each one of the targets so I had a visual reference to their exact position. As soon as Col Mackey and I saw the explosions we were going to employ on them. Things worked out really well because the very first VT round was put down on a weapons cache the Canadians had been trying to identify.

'About 30 seconds later I rolled in, and with a laser spot from my wingman I dropped a GBU-12 on the target. My bomb was followed up by a strafing run by Col Mackey. When my GBU hit, there was a mushroom cloud from the secondaries it set off. That cloud from the effects of my bomb was visible through NVGs for the entire time I remained on station, which was a further nine minutes. The JTAC got on the radio and told us to forget the other four targets and keep on hitting this particular area, along with the adjacent crop fields. So that is what we did. We fired every bullet and every rocket and dropped all of our bombs, except for Col Mackey's GBU-12. At this point I told him to go and find us a tanker, which he did, as we were very low on gas and could not divert into Kandahar.

'When we reached the tanker we discovered that it was equipped with a drogue rather than a flying boom. Now we were in big trouble. We climbed up to 34,000 ft and got our diversionary range charts out, and we both calculated that if we flew at 162 knots at 34,000 ft we could reach Bagram, provided a tanker met us within 50 nautical miles of home. Fortunately, we got the tanker that night and landed safely.

'The notable thing about that sortie was being allowed to take control of the airborne stack, employing eight aircraft within a small target area and controlling artillery fire. Considering the asymmetric nature of the war, the minimal organic firepower the ground guys had and the setup of the ATO, which usually only assigned two aircraft per geographic area, the weight of fire employed in that one kill box was monumental.'

Two days later, on the morning of 4 September, Canadian soldiers from Charles Company, 1st Battalion of The Royal Canadian Regiment were preparing to move forward from their position southeast of the Arghandab River to the objective area on the northeastern side of the river. Following breakfast, the soldiers began to burn their garbage, as was customary, prior to departing at 0700 hrs local. Across the river, a pair of A-10s had arrived to support the Canadian operation, and they were under the control of a Canadian FAC. Their target was to be a building known as the 'White Schoolhouse', which was the centre of Taleban activity in the area. The A-10s were operating at an altitude where daylight was beginning to degrade their NVGs, but the ground was still cast in shadows.

Cleared to employ, the lead A-10 dropped a GBU-12 on the building, while his wingman came in and strafed the fire and smoke from the exploding 500-lb bomb. Having attacked the target several times, the wingman then lost his SA in the changing light conditions and 'padlocked' (locked his gaze) on the garbage fire south of the river, which was lit at about the same time as the LGB exploded and was the same distance away from the A-10 as the 'White Schoolhouse' north of the river. Failing to check his targeting pod or HUD, which would have shown the error, the pilot opened fire. His burst of 30 mm HEI killed Pte Mark Anthony Graham, who was standing next to the fire, and wounded a further 30 soldiers.

KEEPING THE PRESSURE ON

After four months of near ceaseless combat operations, in mid-September 2006 the '384th EFS' was replaced by the 75th FS, which was making the last combat deployment for the A-10 from Pope AFB, North Carolina. The unit arrived at Bagram as the intensity of combat operations had surged past the level of the initial invasion in October 2001 and even Operation *Anaconda*. Arriving as they did shortly after the friendly fire incident involving the A-10, pilots from the 75th FS were thoroughly briefed by their own leadership cadre and senior officers from the 455th AEW on the need to avoid any further fratricidal episodes.

Many of the unit's pilots were making their first combat deployment, including 1Lt Thomas Harney. He recalled the atmosphere at Bagram upon his arrival;

'Obviously anytime something like the friendly fire incident involving the Canadian troops happens it weighs heavily on everybody's heart, and it was an event that nobody wanted to talk about at Bagram. When we arrived on base we were all shown the HUD tape from that flight, and having never been in combat before I found that listening to the radio calls accompanying the video had a sobering effect on me. Despite this obvious distraction, the pilots of the 75th did what they always do – keep focused on our fundamentals. Our leadership cadre told us to concentrate on making the conservative call, when it came to employing ordnance. We needed to be smart, and if there was ever a question over which target to hit, or where it was located, we were to come off dry. Our training

When the 75th EFS relieved the 81st EFS in September 2006, the departing members of the Spangdahlem-bound A-10 unit 'personalised' one of the newly-arrived 'Hogs', adding a gold tooth, a black tooth and eyelashes above a bloodshot eye. As payback, on the morning of the 81st EFS's departure from Bagram, the pilot of 81-0988 found that his jet had been adorned with a chalk rendering of the famous 'Flying Tiger' sharksmouth! (*Capt Tom Harney*)

The 'sharksmouth' easily identifies this A-10 as belonging to the 23rd Wg at Pope AFB, and in this case the 'Tiger Sharks' of the 75th EFS. Tracing its ancestry back to the 1st American Volunteer Group (AVG) in China during the early stages of World War 2, the 'sharksmouth' has adorned aircraft of the 23rd FG ever since. This aircraft is armed with two Mk 82 airburst bombs (with different fusing), a single GBU-12 LGB and an SUU-25 flare dispenser. It also has a Litening pod beneath its starboard wing *(USAF)*

pre-deployment had been built around our very careful understanding of CAS fundamentals. The big focus for us at Bagram was to be smart and save lives, and do it effectively and quickly.'

An effective and quick response to calls for fire would indeed be the situation that faced the unit on 22 September. Indeed, only a matter of minutes passed between the JTAC requesting CAS and the 75th EFS answering the call. Missions flown on this date were typical of those that would dominate the unit's time in-theatre – flying in support of SOF teams in the field. That day, Maj Andrew Stone and his wingman would be providing overwatch for a planned movement by a US Army Special Forces Operational Detachment-Alpha (SFODA) team into a village near Gereshk, in Helmand Province. A month earlier, the same SFODA team had entered the same village and spent five hours in a continuous firefight with Anti-Coalition Militia (ACM).

Through intelligence that had recently been collected, the SFODA team knew that the ACMs were massing for an imminent attack on Coalition forces. Prior to the A-10s arriving, the SFODA ground commander had observed all non-combatants egressing the area, which indicated definite local ACM presence. Maj Stone recalled what happened next;

'Within ten minutes of the JTAC expecting the fight to begin, the SFODA team came into heavy contact with the ACM, as evidenced by his first radio call with M240s and 0.50-cals blazing away in the background. We proceeded to the pre-briefed targets. During our first roll in the JTAC inadvertently bumped the switch on his radio from plain text to secure mode and could not change it back. This meant that both my wingman and I came off dry due to a lack of clearance. I started working with the JTAC to re-establish comms via a series of confirmatory tones – "two beeps for yes" and "many beeps for no". We were able to work out a rudimentary system for clearance authority with the JTAC that allowed us to drop Mk 82 airbursts on cornfields being used by the enemy for concealment of heavy weapons.

'All told, from receiving the call "We are taking fire" to weapons impact took just four minutes, including the dry pass and repositioning for a second run. We attacked five different ACM positions with rockets, GBU-12s, more airbursts and 30 mm rounds over a period lasting just 20 minutes. The JTAC greatly aided our target acquisition by having aim points picked out by mortar rounds. Since we were expending so quickly, I started calling both the CRC [Control and Reporting Centre] and other A-10s that were airborne to let them know that we were about to "Winchester" [run out of ordnance].

'As luck would have it, just as it was time to go to the tanker the JTAC called and told us that he had intel that 300-500 ACM reinforcements were en route. I sent my wingman off to get fuel, coordinating his rejoin with the tanker, while I continued to employ single-ship 30 mm rounds and a self-lased GBU-12. The tanker dragged my wingman back to the target area, and when a break in the action allowed I put him over the target and went to the tanker myself. Upon my return, we employed a few more times until the firing stopped and the ACMs began their retreat.

'By this time the ASOC had sent in more air support, and I soon had two Apaches, a Royal Air Force Harrier GR 7 and a B-1B on station. I "racked and stacked" them, provided AO updates, sent them 9-lines and talked them onto the targets. Eventually I got a call from the CRC

With its refuelling door still open, A-10A 78-0598 of the 75th EFS slides away from a tanker over Afghanistan on 14 December 2006. 'Hogs' worked in pairs over the battlefield, and missions could find them ranging over nearly every corner of the country thanks to aerial refuelling (USAF)

re-tasking my wingman and I to another TIC situation. Departing the area, the JTAC radioed "Thanks for saving our asses today – great job!'"

THE GROVE

On 30 October Maj Stone found himself engaged in the most dynamic CAS mission that he would fly during this deployment. Both he and his wingman would be making 13 gun, rocket and bomb runs within danger-close proximity of friendly troops during a 22-minute period of nonstop action. Maj Stone and his wingman were aware of three on-going TIC situations – 'India Alpha', 'India Bravo' and 'India Charlie' during their pre-flight briefing at Bagram.

'We also had a fist full of air requests – a half-dozen places we were supposed to service during our four- to five-hour mission', Maj Stone explained. 'Our taskings had us working near Kandahar that day. We got airborne and were able to talk to a controller at the ISAF ASOC, which had been stood up on 1 October at Kabul International Airport. He gave us plenty of updates on "who was who in the zoo", and told us to proceed as we were fragged. We headed toward our first AAR, which put us really close to TIC "India Charlie". We steered clear of this firefight, however, so as to deconflict with a B-1B that had gone "Winchester" there a short while earlier.

'We arced away from "India Charlie", and at a distance of about 15 miles from that fight I threw my TGP in there to see if I could spot anything of interest on the ground. I also turned up the strike "freq" to get some SA on what, if anything, was happening. I could only hear the conversation between the crews of two Mirage 2000s that were on station, and it sounded like they were having a heck of a time. My wingman had been on the CRC "freq" while I was on strike, and he got the call re-tasking us to "India Charlie".

The business end of A-10A 80-0277 on the ramp at Bagram AB. Loaded for a mission, the jet carries a single Mk 82 and GBU-12 LGB, as well as a full magazine (1150 rounds) of 30 mm HEI ammunition for the gun (*Capt Tom Harney*)

'We checked in with the JTAC and he gave us the responsibility of "racking and stacking" the "players" in the AO. We were ten miles away from his position – two minutes' flying time. What we figured out in those two minutes was that he needed ordnance. We asked him where he wanted the bombs dropped and he duly described a grove of trees that separated a SFODA team that had been split up during the early stages of the firefight. One group was on the northeastern side of the grove and the other was on the northwestern side, with the JTAC. The group to the northeast had split off from the main team to effect a CASEVAC, as there had been one US soldier KIA. They were headed to a landing zone on the northeastern side of the valley, and although the helicopter had been called there was no ETA available.

'The main SFODA team to the northwest was up on some high ground, having egressed from the grove of trees. I asked the JTAC if he needed ordnance now, or if we had time to do a 9-line brief and a target talk-on. He told me that he needed it now in the grove. We asked him if he had smoke and he said yes, so I told him to have someone in each group pop a canister because I was not going to shoot unless I could do it on either side of the trees. Having seen the smoke, we rolled in and made a couple of strafing passes that seemed to quieten things down and push the ACM back a bit. The JTAC then had us climb up higher and look for additional ACM. For the next 90 minutes we looked for the ACM reinforcements that intelligence assets believed were on their way.

'We continued to look for additional ACM until we started to run low on gas, at which point I tried to get a tanker to come to us but the request was denied. The next call I got was from the JTAC again, as his team was

Tanker fuel has remained critically important for A-10 combat operations throughout OEF. Flying from neighbouring countries in the Persian Gulf and central Asia, KC-135s and KC-10s ploughed through tanker tracks and were instrumental in saving the lives of many American and Coalition soldiers by pushing closer to the fight, allowing the A-10s to refuel often above the engagement they were supporting. Here, an A-10A from the 75th EFS approaches a KC-10 over Afghanistan on 14 December 2006. Interestingly, the jet lacks a Pave Penny pod *(USAF)*

coming under fire once more. What he did not tell me was that the group he was with had moved from their high ground position in order to link up with the soldiers preparing for the CASEVAC. The only way to get to the other team was to go back down into the valley and through the grove of trees, before coming back up the other side. They had rolled back down the track into the middle of the grove, where the team was hammered by the enemy.

'When the JTAC called to say he was taking fire, I still assumed that he was on the northwestern side of the grove. He gave me some coordinates, and when I wrote down the six-digit grid and compared it to the notes I had from the first attack runs, they were different. I queried this with the JTAC, and it was only then that he told me they had moved.

'We were about seven miles west of his location when he called, and I had my wingman rejoin me. As I looked down and saw the world literally exploding, I had no idea where the friendlies were. The JTAC and I had agreed earlier that if they were hit again, each group needed to pop smoke immediately, and that worked well. Having spotted the smoke, we did a 180-degree turn and then started hammering the area. The initial talk-on the JTAC gave us was to "keep the fires west of the fucking road. I need gun-runs north to south now". As these would be danger-close passes, the JTAC gave me his commander's initials, authorising me to employ weapons within danger-close parameters. We could see multiple RPG impacts around the friendly positions.

'On that first pass I moved into a low-angle strafe as the range I was shooting at was just 40 m from SFODA personnel. A low-angle strafe would reduce the bullet dispersion and reduce the possibility of causing fratricide from this attack. We did a couple of passes, moving out a few hundred metres to attack ACM in the grove of trees near a river. We then dropped two Mk 82 airburst a few hundred metres south of the trees in an open area

The 500-lb GBU-12 LGB became available to A-10 units in OEF shortly after jets began arriving in-theatre equipped with Litening targeting pods. The combination of the two meant that for the first time the 'Hog' had the ability to deliver precision-guided munitions (*Capt Tom Harney*)

The grove of trees near Marah, Afghanistan, that was at the centre of the mission flown by Maj Andrew Stone on 30 October 2006. Afghan soldiers who were with the US Army Special Forces that day are seen setting up a defensive position during a break in the fighting. In the 22 minutes that Maj Stone and his wingman were overhead Marah, they fired 1800 rounds of 30 mm ammunition, dropped four 500-lb Mk 82 airburst bombs and one 500-lb GBU-12 LGB and expended six WP rockets *(USAF)*

As the sun sets on Bagram an A-10A of the 75th EFS prepares to takeoff on a night mission in support of ISAF forces. This A-10 is loaded with a Litening targeting pod, two 500-lb Mk 82 airburst bombs, a 500-lb GBU-12 LGB and an SUU-25 flare dispenser *(Capt Tom Harney)*

from where HMGs had been firing. Finally, we targeted the high terrain to the south of the grove with a few more Mk 82s and a GBU-12.

'The two SFODA teams did manage to link back up once the enemy fire had stopped, at which point we handed responsibility for their protection over to "Rammit 43" – a pair of Dutch F-16s. A month later the JTAC from the team was passing through Bagram on his way out of Afghanistan, and he made a point of catching up with me. We sat for three or four hours looking at my films, as well as film he had taken, and we both learned a lot about how the mission had played out.'

AAA FIRE

18 December began as a regular mission for Maj Stone and 1Lt Harney as the 75th EFS's deployment began to wind down. That the intensity of the fighting had continued into December, despite the onset of winter weather, had surprised everyone, and the A-10 pilots were still routinely dropping ordnance. After employing in support of two previous TICs that day, Maj Stone and 1Lt Harney were tasked with supporting a British FOB near Now Zad that had been taking mortar and sniper fire from a valley to the east of the site. The troops had spotted where the militants were located, including some that had fled into a building in an attempt to hide from observation.

'The British soldiers wanted both the mortar position and the building destroyed simultaneously if possible, so that the destruction of one didn't alert the insurgents in the remaining location', explained 1Lt Harney. 'The only problem was that the building being used as an enemy HQ was too large to be taken out by just one LGB. That

was when Maj Stone came up with a plan to take both of them out. I would drop my GBU-12 and he would buddy lase it into the eastern side of the building, immediately after which he would roll in on the mortar team and drop his 500-lb Mk 82 airburst. Finally, I would lase Maj Stone's GBU-12 into the western side of the building. We came in and executed the plan without a pause between strikes, all three bombs hitting their targets.'

'We then reset back into the wheel overhead', Maj Stone recalled, 'and I stacked 1Lt Harney low so we could both use our TGPs simultaneously. We circled above the FOB for a while talking to the JTAC, who soon found some additional folks who had escaped the building between LGB strikes. We targeted them with 30 mm rounds as they were headed west to another compound.

'As we were still doing more TGP searches, looking for any additional "squirters", another team came up on the radio on our Strike "freq" – one

1Lt Tom Harney of the 75th EFS stands in the cockpit of A-10A 79-0206 prior to flying a mission from Bagram on 6 September 2006. He was making his first combat deployment at the time (Capt Tom Harney)

Boasting a typical OEF mission loadout, A-10A 79-0206 of the 75th EFS takes off from the recently repaired runway at Bagram at the start of a dusk CAS on 20 December 2006 (USAF)

A row of 75th EFS A-10As parked
in their revetments at Bagram on
2 December 2006. Snow rarely falls
at the base, and when it does it only
slows A-10 flight operations down,
rather than stopping them altogether
(*Capt Tom Harney*)

that we had not been working on, so it took us a few minutes to sort out
who was calling us. This unknown ground team, who turned out to be
from the Dutch Army, let us know that there were some guys shooting at
us. Okay, fine, so they were shooting at us, which was not all that
uncommon. However, what caught our attention was the fact that every
time we rolled in to make a strafing pass on the "squirters", the guys
targeting us would pull a blanket off of a cart of some sort and fire a
multi-barrelled 12.7 mm ZPU anti-aircraft gun at us as we were coming
off target! They would then throw that blanket over the weapon again as
we were climbing away.

'Apparently the Taleban gunners fired at us a few times before the Dutch
troops, who were on the side of a mountain east of Now Zad, let us know.
We talked to them over the radio, and related this information to the
British JTAC we were working with. It was difficult to pinpoint where
the gun was, so I requested a talk-on between the Dutch team and the
Brit JTAC so as to make sure that we had the right spot. I rolled in and
marked the compound with a rocket, which fell just east of the compound
that I thought I should be aiming for. The Dutch team let me know that
I was targeting the wrong compound, so I moved west to the next
compound. I fired another rocket to confirm that this was my aim point,
the WP hitting the northeastern corner of the walled compound. This
time I had accurately marked the spot where that AAA piece was hidden.'

'I had the only Mk 82 left between us', explained 1Lt Harney, 'so Maj
Stone covered me while I set up on base for the attack. I remember him
telling me that I'd probably see tracers, and to jink accordingly whilst
in-bound so as not to provide too easy a target for the gunners.
Fortunately, his WP rocket had helped suppress the target, as well as mark
it. I rolled in, lined the target up with my HUD's bombing symbology
and "pickled" my LGB at the base of the weapon. I executed my Safe
Escape Maneuver and looked back to make sure I wasn't receiving
fire while I performed my off-target manoeuvring. I saw the familiar
red-orange and smoky blast of the Mk 82 marking the exact spot where
the AAA piece had been located.'

RETURN OF THE 354th

Following a three-month gap that saw Afghan skies bereft of A-10s following the 75th FS's departure for home in January 2007, on 18 April 'Hogs' from the 354th EFS arrived at Bagram. The unit's 12 A-10s would end up flying 2519 sorties totalling 10,051 hours (an average of more than 55 hours of flight time a day) through to October, when the 354th returned to Davis-Monthan. The squadron would fire 153,710 rounds of 30 mm ammunition during its six months at Bagram. These statistics graphically show that ACM forces were still contesting further ISAF expansion into Afghanistan, continuing the fierce resistance they had started a year earlier in 2006.

The 354th FS had been scheduled to deploy later in 2007. However, anxious senior officers in the US Army, realising that there were no A-10s at Bagram and the promised sorties that the USAF had said its Strike Eagles would generate during the spring had not materialised, requested the return of the 'Hog' before the summer fighting season got into full swing.

In 2006 the Taleban had made a strong effort to gain control of the city of Kandahar and many of its surrounding villages. In 2007, the bulk of the fighting would take place in Helmand Province.

Lt Cdr Scott Craig was a US Navy exchange pilot who was making his second Bagram deployment with the 354th. A former SH-60B Seahawk and EA-6B Prowler pilot who had flown sorties over Afghanistan from

After a three-month absence, A-10s returned to Bagram on 17 April 2007 when the first 'Hogs' of the 354th EFS arrived straight from Al Udeid. During the jet's absence in OEF its mission had been fulfilled by F-15E Strike Eagles of the 391st EFS, which was finally allowed to operate from Bagram once the runway re-construction project had been completed in December 2006 *(USAF)*

Hands clear! At the EOR at Bagram an A-10 pilot from the 354th EFS makes his hands visible to the groundcrew as they arm the jet for takeoff. During the 'Bulldogs" 2007 deployment, the squadron flew more than 10,000 combat hours and fired in excess of 150,000 30 mm HEI rounds *(USAF)*

Having all completed 100 combat missions during the 354th's 2007 Bagram deployment, Capt Ryan Cleveland, US Navy exchange pilot Lt Cdr Scott Craig, Capt Daniel Cruz and Maj James Barlow pose on the flightline for a photograph on 5 October 2007. Lt Cdr Craig noted, 'I was exclusively flying nights at the time, and I can remember not being too happy about being woken up to take the picture – and it shows!' *(USAF)*

USS *Carl Vinson* (CVN-70) during the opening phase of OEF in October-November 2001, Lt Cdr Craig was one of the few pilots in the squadron who had in-country experience. Typically, when a squadron rotates in, the pilots who have been there before take the 'new guys' up and show them the ins and outs of flying in Afghanistan. Lt Cdr Craig's first four introduction flights for his squadronmates each ended up with them being called to a TIC!

The 354th's 2007 deployment was to be significantly different to its 2005 tour, when Lt Cdr Craig was last at Bagram. In 2005 he had fired just over 100 rounds of 30 mm ammunition in four months. By the time his six months were over in 2007, he had expended more than 11,000 rounds – just short of what the entire 81st EFS had fired during five months in-theatre in 2003!

The notorious summer thunderstorms had arrived early as Lt Cdr Craig launched with his wingman on a night mission during the first week of May. The storms were raging across most of the country, and aside from another pair of A-10s, no other aircraft were airborne that night that were capable of effecting CAS. A radar altimeter problem forced the first pair of A-10s back to Bagram, leaving Lt Cdr Craig's section as the only aircraft airborne.

'A TIC broke out in Korangal Valley in northeastern Afghanistan', Lt Cdr Craig recalled, 'and we were directed to go and cover it. We tried to reach the valley, but ran into a thunderstorm and had to turn around. We changed altitude and direction and flew back to Bagram, where I set up a holding pattern and pulled out my maps. In the next few minutes I worked out a low-level route so that we could fly 100 miles northeast to Jalalabad, where the JTAC was. We flew at between 1000-1500 ft over ridgelines and down valleys, with a cloud ceiling at 2000 ft. There was

lightning all around us and about three-quarters of an inch of ice on our wings.

'Once we finally reached Korangal Valley I was able to get comms with the JTAC, despite the area still being in the middle of a thunderstorm – I saw numerous lightning strikes. The JTAC got on the radio and told us "Don't come here – extreme weather". I replied, "I copy, and we are here – a two-ship of A-10s overhead. What is the lowdown?" Jalalabad is at the base of the mountain range in which the Korangal Valley is situated. I had the JTAC call up to make sure the troops were still in contact, and they were not. So we ended up returning to Bagram along the same low-level route we had followed to reach Jalalabad.

'It was pretty cool to see that the veteran "Hog" could get airborne and get to where the troops needed us, regardless of the weather.'

'FLIPPER 75'

Operation *Kulang Hellion* was launched on 30 May 2007 when 1st Battalion, 508th Parachute Infantry Regiment, 4th Brigade Combat Team (TF 1 Fury) of the 82nd Airborne Division assaulted Kajaki Sofla – a known Taleban stronghold on the banks of the Helmand River in the northern Helmand Province. This area had seen near ceaseless fighting over the past year.

Capt Andrew Tenenbaum was leading a section of A-10s the afternoon the operation began;

'I was flying as "Scar 11" and Capt Mundy was my wingman. We responded to a TIC south of the Kajaki Dam area. When I checked in there were multiple call signs, and things were quite confusing as nobody was in charge of the air assets. That was the most difficult part of the mission – trying to figure out who else was in the area, as I was told that there were other aircraft operating nearby. I did my best to deconflict so as to ensure that there were no mid-airs, whilst at the same time trying to work out where everybody was on the ground so as to prevent any chance of fratricide. Resolving these issues to our satisfaction prevented us from dealing with the TIC as quickly as we would have liked, however.

'We got pushed over to a JTAC whose call sign was "Doom 06", and he and his men were taking a lot of RPG fire. We put down a WP round and used that as a marker for a series of strafing passes on tree lines from where we could see muzzle flashes emanating. A number of insurgents escaped from the trees into a nearby compound, which my wingman lased

A-10A 80-0278 from the 354th EFS departs Bagram in October 2007, the jet featuring a loadout typical for that time of year when the onset of cooler weather allowed for more ordnance to be carried during takeoff. Interestingly, a Mk 82 500-lb airburst bomb has been affixed to station six (fuselage centreline), which is primarily left unused except for when the jet is carrying an external fuel tank during ferry flights *(USAF)* for me when I targeted it with a GBU-12. We were low on fuel by this point and had to go to the tanker. While we were gone, the 82nd Airborne sent in a flight of CH-47s, one of which was shot down – all seven personnel on board were killed. This was a heart wrenching loss, and I just wished we had been overhead at the time as we could possibly have prevented this from happening. There were no A-10s available to relieve us when we went for fuel.'

'Flipper 75' was the call sign of the CH-47D that was shot down, this helicopter being 'Chalk Two' in a flight of three Chinooks. The helicopter had been struck by a Man-Portable Air Defence System (MANPADS) in the left engine during egress from the HLZ, causing it to crash as it passed over the Helmand River. That night in the same area, patrolling AH-64D Apache crews also reported being shot at by MANPADS.

HOT AUGUST

In August Lt Cdr Craig flew 110 hours exclusively at night, and by October he would be one of four pilots from the 354th EFS who had completed more than 100 combat missions during the deployment. In August, during a typical night sortie, he was 'working a CAS stack of two A-10s and two F-15Es, the Strike Eagles having precision munitions – JDAMs – which they could use for pre-assault fires. For some reason the JTAC could not talk to the F-15Es.

'We had just come off the tanker, and when I checked in with the JTAC he had a town his squad wanted to make an assault on, but some ISR [Intelligence, Surveillance, Reconnaissance] platforms had detected an ambush set up in a line of trees – actually, there were multiple ambushes. The JTAC asked us to come in and hit the enemy with our Mk 82 airbursts, so I quickly took his 9-line brief down while I was still proceeding to my holding point. Although I soon realised that I was going to be over the target 30 seconds late, we still ended up dropping on the line of trees – my wingman and I each used a single Mk 82. We had another platform put an IR marker down, and our bombs hit within three metres of the aim point. So, even though we were using dumb bombs, we were able to put them within the CEP [Circular Error Probable] of a JDAM. BDA was that we got 22 of the 25 enemy waiting to spring the ambush.'

On 13 August Capt Tenenbaum was launched on a CSAR mission to cover the rescue of AH-64 'Capone 20', which had suffered a heavy landing at night in bad weather. The helicopter had come down in high

A-10A 79-0190 taxis into position for takeoff from Bagram AB on 9 June 2007. The 'Hog' is carrying two 500-lb GBU-12 LGBs, a Litening pod, a LAU-131/A rocket launcher and an AN/ARC-235 FACE pod. The latter, fielded for the first time in late 2004, was a solution to communication problems often experienced by aircraft in the mountainous regions of Afghanistan *(USAF)*

terrain northwest of the Khost bowl, which runs along the Khost-Gardez Pass. The crew survived and were ambulatory, although they had a few minor injuries.

'I was flying as "Hawg 17", and we reacted to "Capone 20" going down', explained Capt Tenenbaum. 'I had been off on another tasking, and took over the CSAR effort for the Apache from "Dude 43" – a flight of F-15Es. Intelligence was coming our way, telling us that

This photograph of an A-10 on the ramp at Bagram clearly shows five of the 'Hog's' 11 underwing stations. Station four is loaded with a 500-lb GBU-12 LGB, station five is empty, stations six and eight are loaded with 500-lb Mk 82 airburst bombs and station seven is empty (Capt Tom Harney)

there were enemy forces in the AO that were possibly trying to capture the Apache crew. While all of this was going down, we had "Capone 14" – another Apache – who was trying to get in there and rescue his buddies, crash four-five miles south of "Capone 20", so we now had a double CSAR going on. We had HH-60 Pave Hawks trying to get in there too, but the terrain was just too high for them to reach the downed helicopter.

'We ended up with US Army UH-60 "Daddy 02" landing there, which came as something of a surprise to us. We were always successful when it came to coordinating movements with other Air Force agencies (including the unit flying the HH-60s), but our ability to communicate with Army Aviation assets was not so good. Therefore, when the UH-60 showed up, no kidding I did not even know he was coming until I saw him at the last minute in the AO and he came up on our comm "freq" and we started talking to each other!

'The LZ where "Capone 20" had crashed was not the best, and the Blackhawk was running low on fuel, so the helicopter lowered two of its guys to the ground to help protect the Apache crew and went off to refuel. On their way to the FOB, they were able to pick up the crew of "Capone 14".

'I had been airborne for almost seven hours by this point, so I was relieved by two A-10s and headed home. My replacements oversaw the successful rescue of the crew of "Capone 20".'

Issues with Predator UAVs still existed during the summer of 2007, with a number of A-10 pilots reporting near misses, especially at night.

A-10As belonging to the 354th EFS sit on the ramp at Bagram AB on 28 June 2007. The nearest jet, A-10A 80-0254, was borrowed from the 358th FS so that the 'Bulldogs' had the best available jets for their 2007 deployment. A-10As from the third squadron (357th FS 'Dragons') at Davis-Monthan AFB were also taken on the deployment (USAF)

Procedural problems between manned strike aircraft and UAVs also persisted when it came to prosecuting targets, as Lt Cdr Craig experienced at firsthand;

'We were over a group of friendlies, and a TIC was about to happen according to the intel we had. We had eyes on what we suspected were a group of bad guys, and this was subsequently confirmed as they began to move quickly towards the friendlies. Through ISR, we ascertained that

Taken near the end of the 'Bulldogs" 2007 Bagram tour, 82-0648 shows the wear of a long summer deployment especially around the aircraft's nose, which has been left dirty by gunpowder residue from the gun. The 354th departed Bagram in October 2007, and just as when it had arrived six months earlier, there was no incoming A-10 squadron to turn over duties to *(Scott Craig)*

they had long cylinders on their backs, and received PID that they were the enemy. We were on station, and so was a Predator, and we were targeting this group of eight or nine bad guys in conjunction with a JTAC and a Predator.

'I told the JTAC that if he wanted to employ ordnance he needed to pass us the 9-line as I had eyes on the target – I can roll in with 30 mm in 30-45 seconds. Moments later the Predator operators called in and told the JTAC that he could have a Hellfire immediately, as the UAV was ready to take the shot. The JTAC called me off and broke contact, and in the process of aborting my strafing pass I momentarily lost sight of the target and then had to reacquire it. To me it sounded like the Predator was manned by two guys drinking coffee in a trailer somewhere who were desperate to get a Hellfire shot off. It actually took them more than five minutes to get their Hellfire off, and when it did hit the target it killed just a solitary insurgent – the others scattered. My wingman and I then had to spend the next half-an-hour trying to take out the remaining bad guys who were still moving toward the friendlies. We employed on a couple of them, allowing the Coalition troops to at least break contact.

'I am led to believe that a lot of these procedural problems have been resolved since 2007, but my earlier experiences with Predators put me off working with UAVs.'

ABSENT AGAIN

When the 354th FS departed Bagram in late October 2007, there was no A-10 squadron to replace it. Afghanistan was once again bereft of 'Hogs', as were the ground forces fighting the Taleban on a daily basis. F-15E Strike Eagles from the 336th FS at Seymour Johnson AFB, North Carolina, were now the resident – and lone – CAS aircraft at Bagram. However, on 3 November, when the USAF was forced to temporarily ground its F-15 fleet (including the Strike Eagle) due to a catastrophic in-flight fatigue failure involving an F-15D from the Missouri ANG, the availability of CAS aircraft in OEF was drastically reduced. Strike Eagles were able to sit alert, and launch in emergency situations only. The CAS mission was passed out to other assets.

Recognising the void that had once again been created by the A-10's absence in-theatre, a decision was made to move 'Hogs' from Iraq to Afghanistan. The A-10s involved were part of a 'Rainbow Team' made up of nine jets from the 104th FS of the Maryland ANG and the 172nd FS of the Michigan ANG. Together they formed the 104th EFS. These particular jets were not A-10As that had been in service for nearly 30 years, however. The nine machines flown to Bagram were A-10Cs, and their deployment marked the first time the C-model had seen combat. The 104th EFS was leading the A-10 community into the 21st Century of warfighting capabilities.

The 'Hog' had gone digital.

APPENDICES

A-10 THUNDERBOLT II OEF DEPLOYMENTS 2002-2007

74th EFS 'Flying Tigers'	4 March 2002 – late March 2002
706th EFS 'Cajuns' (706th FS 'Cajuns') (303rd FS 'KC Hawgs')	April 2002 – July 2002
75th EFS 'Tiger Sharks'	July 2002 – September 2002
354th EFS 'Bulldogs'	September 2002 – December 2002
103rd EFS 'Fightin' 103rd'	December 2002 – January 2003
104th EFS 'Maryland Hogs'	January 2003 – June 2003
81st EFS 'Panthers'	June 2003 – November 2003
354th EFS 'Bulldogs'	October 2003 – April 2004
355th EFS 'Fightin' Falcons'	March 2004 – October 2004
81st EFS 'Panthers' (81st FS 'Panthers') (706th FS 'Cajuns')	September 2004 – January 2005
75th EFS 'Tiger Sharks'	January 2005 – May 2005
74th EFS 'Flying Tigers'	May 2005 – September 2005
354th EFS 'Bulldogs'	September 2005 – January 2006
355th EFS 'Fightin' Falcons'	January 2006 – May 2006
81st EFS ('384th EFS') 'Panthers' (81st FS 'Panthers') (303rd FS 'KC Hawgs')	May 2006 – September 2006
75th EFS 'Tiger Sharks'	September 2006 – January 2007
354th EFS 'Bulldogs'	April 2007 – October 2007

COLOUR PLATES

1

A-10A 79-0179 of the 74th EFS/332nd AEG, Jacobabad, Pakistan, March 2002

Delivered to the 23rd TFW in 1980 as A10-0443, this aircraft served with the wing at England AFB until late 1991, when it was transferred to the 507th Air Control Wing at Shaw AFB. Here, it was assigned to the 21st Tactical Air Support Squadron (redesignated the 21st FS in January 1991). During its time at Shaw the 'Hog' also served with the 363rd TFW and the 20th FW between October 1991 and July 1994. The veteran jet was assigned to 23rd FW at Pope AFB in late 1994, and it would make the move to Moody as part of the 23rd FG when the wing was relocated following the 2005 BRAC. Still assigned to the 23rd FG as this book went to press, 79-0179 is depicted here armed with a Mk 82 airburst bomb and an AGM-65D laser Maverick.

2

A-10A 81-0945 of the 74th EFS/332nd AEG, Bagram AB, Afghanistan, March 2002

Carrying the Fairchild-Republic identifier of A10-0640, this 'Hog' was first delivered to the Air Force Flight Test Center (AFFTC) in April 1981. Two years later, it moved to Nellis AFB as part of the 57th FW and Fighter Weapons School. Serving here from October 1983 until May 2000, the 'Hog' then joined the 'Flying Tigers' of the 74th FS and the 23rd Wg at Pope AFB. Four years later, in January 2004, 81-0945 was transferred to USAF Europe (USAFE) and the 81st FS/52nd FW at Spangdahlem AB, Germany, where it currently remains.

3

A-10A 79-0111 of the 706th EFS/455th AEG, Bagram AB, Afghanistan, May 2002

On 23 July 1980 A10-0375 was delivered to the 81st TFW at RAF Bentwaters, where it served until 6 October 1982. Departing the UK, the 'Hog' was transferred to Richards-Gebaur AFB, in Kansas City, Missouri, for service with the US Air Force Reserve, with whom it still remains today. Initially, the jet was assigned to the 303rd FS/442nd TFW, but it would subsequently move to the 706th FS/926th FW, flying out of NAS New Orleans. Following the 2005 BRAC and the devastation of Hurricane 'Katrina', the 706th FS was disestablished and this jet returned to the 303rd FS, now flying from Whiteman AFB. It remains with this unit in 2013. The aircraft is depicted with a LAU-131/A rocket pod beneath its port wing.

4

A-10A 79-0092 of the 706th EFS/455th AEG, Bagram AB, Afghanistan, May 2002

A10-0356 arrived at RAF Bentwaters on 19 June 1980, joining the 81st TFW. The 'Hog' would spend barely two years at the UK base before returning to the USA on 29 July 1982. The jet served with the 303rd FS, flying from Richards-Gebaur AFB and then Whiteman AFB, until it was sent to South Korea and the 25th FS/51st FW at Osan AB in late 2010. The 303rd sent a handful of aircraft (including 79-0092) to augment the 706th FS when it deployed to Bagram in April 2002. As of this writing, the jet remains with the 303rd.

5

A-10A 79-0193 of the 103rd EFS/455th AEW, Bagram AB, Afghanistan, December 2002

A10-0457 began service with the 57th FW at Nellis AFB, and the jet remained here until November 1982 when it was transferred to the 23rd TFW's 76th TFS 'Vanguards' at England AFB. Deploying as part of Operation *Desert Shield*, the jet arrived at King Fahd International Airport in Saudi Arabia on 31 August 1990. After participation in Operation *Desert Storm* in early 1991, the aircraft returned to the USA and was reassigned to the 23rd FW at Pope AFB in April 1992. In January 1995 this jet was transferred to the Pennsylvania ANG's 103rd FS at NAS Willow Grove, and it would remain here until the ANG unit was inactivated in March 2011. 79-0193 is currently serving with the Michigan ANG's 107th FS, based at Selfridge ANGB.

6

A-10A 79-0088 of the 104th EFS/455th AEW, Bagram AB, Afghanistan, February 2003

This aircraft (A10-0352) has spent its entire career with the Maryland ANG's 175th FW at Warfield ANGB, the jet being part of the first group of 'Hogs' to commence service with the wing when the 104th TFS switched from the A-37B to the A-10A on 3 October 1980.

7

A-10A 81-0954 of the 81st EFS/455th AEW, Bagram AB, Afghanistan, June 2003

A10-0649 commenced its first assignment on 25 October 1982 when it began service with the 92nd TFS 'Skulls' of the 81st TFW. Initially incorrectly serialled 81-0016, this error was soon fixed to reflect the correct serial designation. Following the inactivation of the 81st TFW, this jet was transferred to the 510th TFS/52nd FW at Spangdahlem AB in January 1993. It then became part of the 81st FS following the inactivation of the 510th FS in April 1994. The jet would remain with USAFE until August 2008, when it was transferred to the ANG/AFRC Test Center at Davis-Monthan AFB.

8

A-10A 82-0650 of the 81st EFS/455th AEW, Bagram AB, Afghanistan, June 2003

On 20 September 1983 A10-0698 commenced its operational career with the 510th TFS 'Buzzards' as part of the 81st TFW. The jet moved with the 510th TFS to Spangdahlem AB in January 1993 and was transferred to the newly reactivated 81st FS in February 1994. The 'Hog' is still assigned to the 81st FS/52nd FW in 2013.

9

A-10A 81-0943 of the 354th EFS/455th AEW, Bagram AB, Afghanistan, November 2003

Arriving at RAF Bentwaters on 19 August 1982, A10-0638 wore the wrong serial number for several months, being mistakenly identified as 81-0005. As part of the 81st TFW, the jet belonged to the 92nd TFS 'Skulls' until it was transferred back to the USA in May 1992 following the inactivation of the A-10 units at RAF Bentwaters. Since returning home the 'Hog' has remained with the 355th FW at Davis-Monthan AFB, where it has served with the three frontline squadrons within the wing. 81-0943 is currently serving with the 358th FS 'Lobos', one of the two training squadrons on base. The aircraft is depicted here carrying a Litening pod, as well as a LAU-131/A and GBU-12.

10

A-10A 80-0204 of the 354th EFS/455th AEW, Bagram AB, Afghanistan, February 2004

Illustrated wearing the markings of the 357th FS 'Dragons' (another A-10 training squadron based at Davis-Monthan AFB), this jet was selected to deploy with the 354th EFS in late 2003. 80-0204 remained in 'Dragons'' colours throughout its time at Bagram. Originally delivered as A10-0554 to the 81st TFW's 91st TFS 'Blue Streaks' at RAF Bentwaters, the jet was eventually transferred to the 355th FW at Davis-Monthan AFB in May 1992. The aircraft is presently serving with the 66th Weapons Squadron at Nellis AFB.

11

A-10A 80-0281 of the 81st EFS/455th AEW, Bagram AB, Afghanistan, November 2004

On 29 July 1982 A10-0631 became part of the 81st TFW's 92nd TFS 'Skulls' at RAF Bentwaters. Following the wing's inactivation on 1 July 1993, the jet served with the 355th FW at Davis-Monthan AFB until September 2002. The airframe would then spend seven years with the 81st FS/52nd FW at Spangdahlem AB, before once again returning to the USA. Since September 2009, the 'Hog' has served with the 303rd FS/442nd FW of the AFRes, flying from Whiteman AFB. This aircraft is depicted carrying an AN/ARC-235 Fighter Aircraft Command & Control Enhancement (FACE) pod. Fielded for the first time in late 2004, the FACE pod was a solution to communication problems often experienced by aircraft in the mountainous regions of Afghanistan.

12

A-10A 80-0232 of the 81st EFS/455th AEW, Bagram AB, Afghanistan, November 2004

A10-0582 was delivered to the 81st TFW at RAF Bentwaters on 29 January 1982. In September 1990 the 'Hog' returned to the USA, moving to the Pennsylvania ANG's 111th Tactical Air Support Group (TASG) at NAS Willow Grove. Five years later, in April 1995, the jet was transferred to the 706th FS/926th FW of the AFRes at NAS New Orleans. This aircraft was one of six A-10s sent by the 706th to Bagram to augment the 81st FS from September 2004. 80-0232 remains with the 706th FS today, although the unit now calls Nellis AFB home.

13

A-10A 80-0252 of the 75th EFS/455th AEW, Bagram AB, Afghanistan, February 2005

This A-10 (A10-0602) was first delivered to the 51st TFW at Suwon AB, where it served from November 1982 until October 1987. Following its spell in South Korea, the jet served with the 354th TFW at Myrtle Beach AFB, South Carolina, until July 1992, when it moved to Pope AFB and the 23rd FW. The aircraft is still serving with the 75th FS today, the unit having called Moody AFB home since October 2006.

14

A-10A 78-0597 of the 74th EFS/455th AEW, Bagram AB, Afghanistan, August 2005

Although still assigned to the 75th FS, and wearing the squadron's markings, this jet was actually flown by pilots from the 74th EFS from May 2005 after the latter unit replaced the 'Tiger Sharks' at Bagram. Rather than deploying new aircraft from Pope AFB, the 74th simply assumed ownership of its sister-squadron's A-10s in Afghanistan. A10-0217 had been delivered to RAF Bentwaters on 21 June 1979 for service with the 81st TFW, but it was soon transferred to the 354th TFW at Myrtle Beach AFB on 7 July 1983. Following the deactivation of the 354th TFW at Myrtle Beach AFB in March 1993, 78-0597 was transferred to the 75th FS/23rd Wing at Pope AFB, with whom it remains as of this writing.

15

A-10A 81-0939 of the 354th EFS/455th AEW, Bagram AB, Afghanistan, October 2005

Originally given the serial 81-0001 and delivered as such, A10-0634 arrived at RAF Bentwaters on 29 July 1982 and was soon re-serialled to reflect the correct number. This 'Hog' was assigned to the 511th TFS 'Vultures', and when RAF Bentwaters became overcrowded the 511th TFS was transferred to the 10th TFW at RAF Alconbury on 1 September 1988. The jet arrived in Saudi Arabia at King Fahd International Airport on 27 December 1990 as part of the 354th TFW (Provisional), supporting Operation *Desert Shield* and then participating in Operation *Desert Storm*. During ODS on 21 January 1991, the jet suffered light AAA damage, but safely returned to King Fahd. On 12 May 1991 the aircraft returned to RAF Alconbury but soon moved on to the 507th TACW, which became the 363rd TFW and then the 20th FW at Shaw AFB. In April 1993 the 'Hog' was transferred to the 355th FW at Davis-Monthan AFB, where it currently belongs to the 357th FS.

16

A-10A 79-0187 of the 355th EFS/455th AEW, Bagram AB, Afghanistan, February 2006

A10-0451 initially served with the 23rd TFW at England AFB as part of the 74th TFS 'Flying Tigers'. It too deployed in support of Operation *Desert Shield*, arriving at King Fahd International Airport on 2 September 1990. On 21 May 1991, following Operation *Desert Storm*, the jet left Saudi Arabia for England AFB. Shortly after returning home the 'Hog' was transferred to the 917th TFW of the AFRes, flying out of Barksdale AFB. From June 1995 to June 2006 this jet served with the 355th FS/354th FW at Eielson AFB, Alaska. Following the 2005 BRAC, the 355th FS was deactivated and 79-0187 was delivered to the 354th FW. It remains with the wing today, flying with the 357th FS.

17

A-10A 81-0995 of the 355th EFS/455th AEW, Bagram AB, Afghanistan, April 2006

First serving with the 343rd TFW at Eielson AFB, A10-0690 then became part of the 354th FW's 355th FS. During its time in Alaska the jet was adorned with special markings as depicted here – nose art, full-colour fin tips and shaded wing and unit codes. Following the deactivation of the 355th FS in 2006 the A-10 was transferred to the 23rd FG, and it is currently serving with the group's 75th FS.

18
A-10A 81-0963 of the 81st EFS/455th AEW, Bagram AB, Afghanistan, June 2006
Delivered to RAF Bentwaters on 20 September 1983 as part of the 92nd TFS 'Skulls' of the 81st TFW, this jet would spend nearly a decade flying from the UK before being moved to the 52nd FW to serve with the newly reactivated 510th TFS 'Buzzards' at Spangdahlem AB. In February 1994, the jet made the transition to the 81st FS, and it remained at the German base until 1 April 2011 when A10-0658 crashed near Laufeld, Germany and was destroyed. The pilot, Lt Col Scott Hurrelbrink, ejected safely after becoming disorientated whilst descending in formation in thick cloud prior to landing at Spangdahlem.

19
A-10A 82-0649 of the 81st EFS/455th AEW, Bagram AB, Afghanistan, August 2006
On 20 September 1983 A10-0697 was delivered to the 81st TFW at RAF Woodbridge. Part of the 91st TFS 'Blue Streaks' until February 1992, the jet moved to the 510th TFS at Spangdahlem AB, Germany, on 29 January 1993 as part of the 52nd FW. Making the transition to the 81st FS 'Panthers' in February 1994, this A-10 still serves at the German base.

20
A-10A 79-0110 of the 81st EFS/455th AEW, Bagram AB, Afghanistan, August 2006
Delivered to RAF Bentwaters and the 81st TFW on 19 June 1980, A10-0374 spent two years at the UK base. On 1 June 1982 it joined the AFRes' 303rd FS at Richards-Gebaur ARB. This aircraft was one of six A-10s sent by the 303rd to Bagram to augment the 81st FS from May 2006. As of this writing the jet is still with the 303rd.

21
A-10A 78-0631 of the 81st EFS/455th AEW, Bagram AB, Afghanistan, August 2006
A10-0251 was delivered to the 81st TFW at RAF Bentwaters on 28 September 1979, and it subsequently spent three years at the base. It was then transferred to the AFRes and the 303rd FS at Richards-Gebaur ARB on 11 June 1982. Since then, the jet has remained with the 303rd FS, and it has since moved with the unit to Whiteman AFB, where it currently still serves. Like 79-0110, 78-0631 was also assigned to the 81st FS at Bagram in 2006.

22
A-10A 78-0598 of the 75th EFS/455th AEW, Bagram AB, Afghanistan, November 2006
Delivered to the 354th TFW at Myrtle Beach AFB in December 1979, A10-0218 served with the wing until August 1992 when it was transferred to the 23rd Wg at Pope AFB. The 'Hog' spent nearly 18 years with the 23rd Wg and then the 23rd FG, moving between the 74th and 75th FSs, before being sent to the Indiana ANG to serve with the 163rd FS of the 122nd FW in May 2010. The jet remains with the squadron as of this writing.

23
A-10A 79-0139 of the 75th EFS/455th AEW, Bagram AB, Afghanistan, November 2006
This jet was delivered to the 23rd TFW from the factory, although A10-0403 only served at England AFB for a short time before moving to Davis-Monthan AFB in late 1979 to join the recently formed 355th Tactical Training Wing. Myrtle Beach AFB and the 354th TFW was the next stop for 79-0139, the A-10 spending three years at the base before moving to Pope AFB and the 23rd Wg in June 1992. Since then it has served exclusively with the 75th FS 'Tiger Sharks'.

24
A-10A 82-0648 of the 354th EFS/455th AEW, Bagram AB, Afghanistan, May 2007
A10-0696 spent most of its early years with the 3246th Test Wing at Eglin AFB. From May 1990 until January 1992 it was with the 23rd TFW at England AFB, before being transferred to the 354th FW at Davis-Monthan AFB, where the jet has remained ever since. Serving with all three squadrons during its tenure at the Arizona base, the jet has most recently been assigned to the 354th FS. It is depicted here in 358th FS markings, the aircraft being borrowed by the 354th for its 2007 Bagram deployment.

ACKNOWLEDGEMENTS

The author would like to thank the following individuals for their invaluable help in writing this book – Brig Gens John 'Horndog' Horner and Ronald 'Bruce' Miller, Cols Matt 'El Cid' Neuenswander, Scott 'Soup' Campbell, Andra 'Poptart' Kniep, Keith 'Marty' McBride, Brian 'Borg' Borgen and Wade Thompson, Lt Cols Andrew 'FATTS' Stone, Mark 'Darth' Gilchrist, Anthony 'Crack' Roe and David 'D-Ray' Raymond, Majs John 'Beercan' Collier, Mathew 'Fumble' Robins, David 'Rox' Kirkendall, Barry 'Sluf' Coggins and Andrew Tenenbaum, Capt Tom 'PETA' Harney and Cdr (ret.) Scott Craig. The help provided by Doug Dildy was also essential, as was the support given to me by my family, namely Stefanie, Carsten, Madison and especially Jamison.

INDEX

References to illustrations are shown in **bold**.
Plates are on the pages prefixed pl, with
corresponding captions on the page in brackets.